Published By Buttonwillow Press

ORDER COPIES FROM

Buttonwillow Civil War Dinner Theater

Post Office Box 37, Whitwell, TN 37397

www.CivilWarDinnerTheater.com

This book is dedicated to our kin:
Pvt. Jonathan Browning, 43rd Mississippi Infantry,
CPL. Everett (Elly) Brisbane Glisson, Pee Dee Rangers,
10th South Carolina,
Pvt. W. P. (Billy Bugler) Richardson, Gregg's Company,
McQueen's Light Artillery,
Pvt. David Glisson, Swamp Fox Guards,
10th South Carolina,
Pvt. James (Jempsey) R. Lewis,
10th South Carolina Infantry, Co F.

GOD SAVE THE SOUTH!

TABLE OF CONTENTS

FORWARD

"Tradition usually rests upon something which men did know; history is often the manufacture of the mere liar."
Jefferson Davis

My name is Steve Gipson, and I am all about tradition; Southern Tradition and American Tradition, both being the same.

Tradition reflects a time-worn, time-tested process that we have to have to weather the extreme climate that a kinetic society demands. Without tradition, we drift. History records the events that tradition creates. I try to gather that history and re-tell it in a way that my readers will understand and be entertained by.

I don't mean to lie on purpose, but, as Mr. Davis indicated, I will end up fibbing about something because I might get the facts wrong; no one knows the whole story about any time in history. Even as current events unfold, modern journalists can get their facts mixed up; try interviewing three witnesses to a car crash and see where that gets you.

I am not a well-known historian; as a matter of fact, this is my first book. I have been on stage presenting this material for a long time, so, I guess I have a small following. I do not have a degree in history from any university; I am, however, co-owner of the Buttonwillow Civil War Dinner Theater, located in Tennessee, which qualifies me to act like I have a degree. (I own the parts that the public never sees. Allison, my wife, owns all of the pretty parts.)

Allison is a historian, too. She is brilliantly funny. We do the shows together on stage in our little dinner theater where we see people from all over the world. We are both trying hard to figure out what happened. We are self-educated, self-motivated, and absolutely astounded at the silliness that passes for history in our public institutions.

I guess we have to ask this question early on in this exploration: where has the use of logic disappeared to? The story of The War Between the States is taught in such a way that baffles anyone with any sense of reason.

Case in point; why would so many Southern soldiers sacrifice so much for something they had nothing to do with? Consider that statistics indicate that about 26% of the South held slaves in 1860; that means that 74% did not. There is no way that the South could have raised their fighting numbers to the level they did using only 26% of their population. So, that means people who did not own slaves had to be part of that number. If they had no vested interest in Slavery, then, logically, that would mean that they had other reasons for their actions.

Why, then, would anyone believe that this War was about slavery alone? Come on, folks, let's dig deeper and have some fun with this.

I am a firm believer that God grants us all special talents and He granted me a deep curiosity; He also gave me the ability to tell stories. That combination of gifts resulted in the play that I wrote called "Granddaddy's Watch". After 38 years of producing shows on the road, my passion for this period finally found a path that led me to this little theater, Allison, and this production.

Most of the folks who will read this have been to our theater and have seen the play that I wrote. This book re-plays most of what one saw. It is the result of so many requests from our visitors to put this down in writing so that they could take it home, and have more time to absorb the vast flow of information that they witnessed at our theater. For those who have not seen what we do on stage, this will serve to tell the story of what happened in America that brought us to war. So, either way, this book will satisfy both markets for what we do. I will try my best to get this close.

The Constitution plays a major role in this story. The life or death of this great nation depended on its restoration and consideration in all that had transpired. Tennessee's own involvement in this great struggle is part of that tale. The play involves a brother and sister from East Tennessee. They meet by accident at his Union camp, and end up arguing like 8 year-olds. The material in the play is taken from historical sources and is a balanced look at both sides.

Remember, all Southerners were not pro-Confederate, just as all modern Southerners are not Democrats or Republicans. This fact will start a debate with some, I know, but I am convinced that one would be hard-pressed to claim that all of their ancestors took up one side or the other in this conflict; I have been to too many family re-unions. (Some of you have seen our latest family re-union on COPS.)

Southerners know very well that we can't settle on a single S.E.C. football team in the fall; just count the dead in the parking lot after a blow-out in an Auburn-Alabama game. Why, then, believe that all of your ancestors were for the destruction or preservation of our Union? It isn't logical. There are always gray areas even in matters such as the War Between the States.

Eastern Tennessee had deep roots in the formation of our early nation. That is why it provided so many volunteers to the Union army (close to 51,000). (Point of trivia: The nick-name for Tennessee is "The Volunteer State", a name that evolved during the War of 1812.)

That figure of 51,000 was a lot larger than it may seem, considering the entire Tennessee population in 1860 was only 826,722 Whites, 275,719 Slaves, 7,300 Free Blacks; totaling

1,109,741. That figure also represents the entire state, and the 51,000 came just from the Eastern section. Read those figures, again. I know it may have lost you. There was a lot of Union sympathy in areas of the South....a lot.

I know that some of this information is going to hurt some feelings because it goes against what you were told or thought. It is going to confuse some, and absolutely confound others. I have to admit that some of it confounded me. Please, be open, look hard at the facts, and look this stuff up, if you have to.

We all know that our educational system has been over-run, in great part, by a lunacy called "political correctness". This cancer stifles the truth, discourages discourse, and drives us further apart. This book will try to link us back into a dialogue with a free-flow of fresh information and a positive end-game. If the reader is not willing to discuss issues, then don't read another word of this. If you subscribe to "political correctness", check yourself into the nearest treatment center, hug a tree, and leave all of us alone, please. We cannot continue this censorship and survive.

Our American educators are wearing the handcuffs of suppression in a nation that was born out of it; that is the irony that we, as Americans, are faced with. Our right of Free Speech doesn't exist, really, because of the undercurrent of this social malady. Any censorship means total censorship; one cannot be "a little pregnant". We either have *Freedom of Speech* or we don't, there is no middle ground.

When, one must ask, did it become "wrong" in America to express one's beliefs? We are constantly badgered with a social censorship that would make our Founding Fathers cringe. Free Speech and the Right to Protest is our heritage, and I will speak my mind, as you should; I will publish this book, and stand back to see how much trouble I get into. Ya'll pray for me, this nation, and our kids. We are going to need His help more every day.

It was, after all, a Southerner named Jefferson Finis Davis who

14

had so much of this figured out so long ago. He and other Southerners could see the corruption of this system long before it came slamming into us. Jefferson Finis Davis was right.

Davis once said, "Our situation illustrates the American idea that governments rest on the consent of the governed, and that it is the right of the people to alter or abolish them whenever they become destructive of the ends for which they were established." Does this not sound familiar?

With the "politically correct" shadow smothering the issue of slavery, we are bound and gagged from discussing the sensitive issues; we are attacked for asking for the truth. You have to ask yourself the question, "What is it in our history that some folks want to keep from us?" What are these narrow-minded politicians and special-interest groups so frightened of?

Avoiding real history in order to keep from hurting someone's feelings is a moral crime, in my view, and is even more dangerous to us as society in the final tally. It really smacks of political corruption and an effort to sway our youth toward the Left. The instruction of history should not include any contemporary political leanings, right or left. We need to edit political-thinking out of the pages of our school books once and for all. Tell the kids the truth; they will work it out just fine. Lie to them early, and they become jaded, and disinterested in the well-being of their own nation. Teach a little "Americanism" for a start.

There seems to be more of an assault on our Constitution today than most people seem to be aware of and "political-editing" in our public educational system is one way that it is being done.

Avoiding real truth in history only serves to drive a bigger wedge between groups, creating a lack of trust. We are now paying the price in several ways, including a lack of civic pride in our young people. Who are our kid's heroes?

We are constantly bombarded with demands for diversity, so

15

here you go; this book will bring a lot of real diversity back to the table. It will, however, be in a way most of you are not going to expect. I follow no one's rule on how to couch this, be ready for a frontal assault on "bias".

It is a fact that the history in this nation was written by Whites for Whites for nearly 200 years. People of Color were left out for several reasons: racism, bigotry, ignorance, prejudice, forgetfulness, and a plain lack of just paying attention to the facts. We will insert those groups back into the picture as they should have been a long time ago; you may be surprised at just how mixed a group we were, and how different we all were.

For the "politically correct" crowd, this will get hairy. This group does not want to acknowledge the involvement of Blacks or Hispanics in slavery, racism or bigotry. Their focus is on all of the "evil" propagated by White Europeans, alone. Well, that group is going to have to step aside, go drink a $6.00 bottle of imported water, and catch the next "Feel-Good" talk show while we untangle their mess; it is time for a reality check.

I am not writing this book for the entire nation, I am writing it for those who have some common sense and a semblance of Christian morality. I also believe that they are still the majority.

Any nation or people who cannot face their past will never have a future. Let us move forward with or without the help of those on the Left; they have their forums, we have ours.

Any educator who might be reading this book, take note: you really were not told the whole story about this War, our history, or the complex issues that caused the frictions and arguments. The universities you attended used to stand for free-thought, open-questions, impartial probing, and a true political diversity. That has come to a screaming halt in most cases due to pressure by special interest groups, minority groups, and a few questionable professors long on tenure and short on common sense. The continuing lack of real moral leadership from the school administrators only makes it harder for America to regain its honor, respect and tradition.

People run and duck when someone yells "racist". Now, it is time to make a stand. Try standing your ground with facts and let the foolish reveal themselves. Remember that name-calling doesn't work on people of real honor. My grandfather always told me to remember what Davy Crockett said, "Be sure that you are right, then, go ahead." Davy was a Southerner, too.

In summary, I believe that education should be held sacred; educators should be held to a higher standard and an obligation to the truth. They should be our children's role models.

When our history became a political football, we began to lose our tradition; history by consensus is called "fiction".

All in all, the word "education" is what my Grandfather used to refer to as a "75 cent word for learning stuff", that's all. It comes from life's lessons, one's personal experiences, some from reading, some from what we are told, and some from a sixth sense. The term "education" has become almost too sanctimonious for its own good, and needs to be freshly challenged by a new crop of teachers. People who use their degrees to bluntly push their political agenda are not real educators, they are activists. These folks are guaranteed their right to speak, but not from the front of a classroom full of public school kids who cannot have a say in the matter. The status quo in education has to come to an end. A degree becomes mute if it represents a falsehood.

It is important to understand that everything that you read is not true; it doesn't matter how lettered that author is. Some of the most learned men in their times had influential clout and taught facts that have been proved utter nonsense. Yet, in their day, they were the ones that everybody looked to. You might remember when our best scholars were convinced that our earth was flat; same folks believed that the earth was the center of the universe.

Since I don't have any degrees, there will be a lot of folks who will dismiss me altogether. Those are the people that see the package and not what's in it.

When it comes down to it, all education is "self-taught". Reading and researching on one's own volition or being made to read something in a formal situation creates the same results. One does not have to be "formally educated" to know what they know. Lincoln's formal education is estimated to be around 18 months, taken over a period of years. The "Education Establishment" is like a lot of labor unions; it protects itself with this self-serving idea that one has to be sanctioned by them, or you don't count; really? I believe that we all count. I have never met anyone of any intellect that I couldn't learn something from.

Truth is not exclusive to the majority, it is what is it is.

Let us now explore the reason that most people believe what they read in those universities. It's all predicated, in a large part, on something that happened in history a long time ago. Let us now see how history can teach history.

Please note: In my humble opinion, we are the monkeys in the cage of life.... so, come on, grab a banana, and find out what they didn't tell you. Let's get "educated"!

POST FORWARD

JOHANNES GUTENBERG

Henne Gänsfleisch zur Laden, AKA "Johannes Gutenberg", played a big part in this peculiar way of looking at the printed word; this is when mankind took the giant leap into the absurd.

Before Gutenberg invented the first workable printing press in 1440, all documents were hand-written and hand-copied. Books and manuscripts were rare and incredibility expensive. At that time, few people could even read.

Gutenberg began by printing assorted materials for the Catholic Church...then, took up the project of printing Bibles....a lot of Bibles.

It is difficult to think of printed materials today as rare, considering the massive amounts of junk mail that we receive. In 1440, printed materials did not exist....until Mr. Gutenberg started churning out his stuff. The landfill assault began in earnest in the mid-15th century.

When anybody, at that time, saw something that was printed, they believed that it had to be the Gospel...therefore, it had to be true. Ergo, "If its writ, it's right". (Yankee translation for our Northern readers: "If it is written, then it has to be truth.") For years, printed materials were exclusively religious and not to be dismissed. That concept of "truth" was to last for centuries.

You know that most people in high school slept through their history class... and for good reason. At the tender age of fourteen or fifteen, most of us were looking to the opposite sex for attention, and really zoned out when the history teacher, most likely a football coach, was trying to bore us with information that meant nothing to us. Young people have no real life-experience and cannot relate to this kind of material. The old adage "Education is wasted on the youth." is absolutely right on the mark.

This book is a combination of hard facts, quotes and trivia that I have discovered; my opinions and observations are sprinkled throughout. I have no illusions that I know everything, and I am ready to look hard at any point the reader might offer about a difference of opinion.

The reader must know that I have come to the conclusion that no one has all of the facts about this War, least of all, me. I have read other opinions of historical matter that I personally do not agree with, just as you have. The reader of this book may well find the same with what I propose; fair enough.

What I will try to do is tell a story of what I believe happened in the past and do what I can to make it all make sense.

If my sense of humor helps in this narrative, then that makes it all the better. If the reader is looking for another dry "fact-by-fact" account of American history, one might just as well put this down now. There will be serious and complicated parts in this, but, since you are not being forced into reading something you don't want to, take your time. I find a lot of coffee helps stir the mind thru the "info-assaults".

If you are still reading this, then we are on the way to see just what occurred in this country that has so many baffled and confused and eager to defend or rebuke. I find that real history and social history to be like night and day; this book reveals why.

I am a Southerner, and I make no apologies for that; it will explain my passion on certain subjects. My parents, too, were Southerners, and God saw fit to hatch me in Huntsville, Alabama; for that, I will always be grateful........ God Save the South!

ALABAMA CAPITOL BUILDING 1861

"Truth will ultimately prevail where there is pains taken to bring it to light."

GEORGE WASHINGTON, A Southerner,

Farewell Address to the People of the United States

CHAPTER ONE

THE SET-UP FOR A CATSTROPHY

Anyone, who takes on the task to somehow explain the causes of The War Between the States, deserves the consequences and the debates that will follow. A lot of people that I run into have read just enough to know less than they did before they read it; they are experts born out of a paragraph off of the internet, or a discussion thru an alcohol-fogged conversation with somebody behind the local snack bar back in high school; quality sources, no doubt. They are going to have a "hissy fit" with some of this.

It is probably safe to say that one of the original causes of The War Between the States was when a Dutch ship landed off the coast of Virginia in 1619 and off-loaded a cargo of African slaves at Jamestown. This occasion will set into motion a debate and a cancer that will engulf our nation later. It will take almost 250 trying years for it to develop into a war, but that simple boatload of Africans was probably a major key that will play a role in the violence that will erupt in 1861 in South Carolina. That is not to say other factors were not quickly added which would make this a plausible scenario, but it was a doozy. Slavery alone, I believe, would not have been enough, in itself, to bring us to war; it will involve other complications. History is full of complications.

To give it a Southern analogy, "It is akin to making a cake; the basic ingredients being the base, the final flavor will be determined by any additional flavorings you add. A touch of cinnamon versus a pinch of ginger or a dash of lemon concentrate... and the end results are altered unmistakably."

I propose that the differences between the kinds of folks who landed early on made up that mix. You have heard the expression, "We are a melting pot."... well, I think we are more of a "cake mix". I don't think we ever actually melted together completely.

By the eve of this Great War, numerous sectional arguments had grown in number and scope to a point that Southerners were absolutely convinced that Northerners, like Negroes or Asians, were of a different race. (I use the term "Negroes" as a historical reference, which I will do whenever I am writing about any Minority in the time. This nomenclature is vital to the full comprehension of the subject. Inserting "politically correct" names for groups dilutes and constricts us from fully understanding the cultural reality of the time. In other words, Africans were not referred to as African-Americans at this time.)

It isn't clear who started this peculiar idea about the differences between the races; later on, though, great Southern leaders will buy into it and promote it freely and openly. People saw everything in a different light in those days, please understand. You have to remove yourself from your computer and sit in a carriage for just two hours. Realities change, and so do perceptions. You are not your ancestors by any stretch.

(Point of trivia: Deaths from dental abscesses today are so rare, that it is difficult to fathom that only 200 years ago, this was a leading cause of death. When the London (England) "Bills of Mortality" began listing the causes of death in the early 1600's, "teeth" were continually listed as the fifth or sixth leading cause of death. This does not include the category of "Teething", which was probably erroneously blamed for many children's deaths. As we examine several historic factors of this period, it is apparent that the number of deaths attributed to "teeth" in the seventeenth and eighteenth centuries was probably fairly accurate.)

A case in point about this "peculiar difference" was an idea promoted by Admiral Raphael Semmes of the Confederate Navy; he was associated with the Confederate Ship CSS *Alabama*. He proclaimed, with public vigor, that the North was populated by descendants of "the cold Puritan Roundheads of Oliver Cromwell"—who had overthrown and executed the King of England in 1649. Others of that lot had fled to Holland, got themselves booted out of there, and ended up landing at Plymouth, Massachusetts. Yep, the Puritans were certainly the party hounds of their day. Reputations do follow you.

Southerners were, according to theory, "descended from enemies of Cromwell." They were the "gay cavaliers".

(Please note a small lesson within a point: The word "Gay" in the sixteenth and seventeenth century had nothing to do with one's sexual proclivities. This illustrates an on-going problem with contemporary history and the definition changes of words. "Gay", like a lot of words, has been through a lot of changes...and if one was to read about "gay cavaliers" in our public schools today, one would assume that they were homosexual, when they were not openly espousing any sexual preference. We now have a new generation of teachers who are not old enough to remember the older definition of "gay". Ask them what a "45" was in 1965...they would probably say it was a gun. (If you really don't know, it was a 45 RPM record...rock on!)

These "gay cavaliers", as they were called, had given Southerners an easy-going and chivalrous demeanor, somehow. These Southern aristocrats were living their own version of King Arthur's Camelot. Now, delete the word "serfs" and insert the words "slaves" and "poor white trash". These folks fed off of the plantation system; it really reflected a reality in the Old South.

Admiral Semmes stated, and believed, that Northerners had "evolved into gloomy, saturnine (sic), (melancholy or sullen), and fanatical people," who "seemed to repel all the more kindly and generous impulses." Semmes overlooked the fact that Georgia had been settled by convicts, Louisiana by deportees, and his wife was from Ohio. I guess we should be honest here and say that people see what they want to, don't they? Isn't that why arguments start? You bet; "Everybody is crazy except me and the monkey that lives in my pants!"... it was that kind of reasoning.

How these beliefs about Northerners came to pass between 1619 and 1860 illustrates the astonishing capacity of human nature to confound the situation, and justify what had become unjustifiable; repeat a partial truth long enough, and people grow to accept it as fact. These tidbits are the "urban legends".

Slavery spread from one colony to the other and was built into all of their economies to one degree or another. All of the original thirteen colonies were involved in slavery... all of them. This piece of information is left out by our friends on the Left, who don't want anyone knowing that there had been slaves in such paragons of Human Justice as Vermont and New Hampshire. This truth will indeed complicate matters later, as well. Since everyone had a hand in slavery to some degree, disagreements regarding its abolition will be handled on a more regionally-centered basis later; and that will morph into a sectional crisis which will go national. This gets even better and more complicated.

By the turn of the nineteenth century, slavery was confined mostly in the South where the economy was agricultural. There were fewer practical uses for slaves in the North, where most slaves were used as domestics or on small family farms. Large farms, or plantations, did not evolve in the Northern colonies to any degree. The fact is that, for a while, it looked like slavery was going to play out on its own. Thomas Jefferson probably summed up the attitude of the day when he described the South's "peculiar institution" as a "necessary evil"; but he had to know that it would just be matter of time when human labor would be replaced by machines. Thomas Jefferson would have been the catalyst for such machinery himself. His ability to design labor-saving devices still astounds me. (Go see Monticello sometime; it is worth the trip.)

Ironically enough, it was a real Yankee, born and educated in the North, who will play the next key role in bringing this war to America. His invention was not a military one, rather, a device that would spur the production of a crop that would cause the slave population to sky-rocket; introducing Eli Whitney.

ELI WHITNEY

Having traveled south for employment, Whitney ended up at Mulberry Grove Plantation, located near Savannah, Georgia. This large plantation was the home of Mrs. Catherine Greene, the widow of Revolutionary War hero, Nathaniel Greene. It was there, with the aid of Mrs. Greene, that he developed the "cotton gin" ("gin" was short for "engine" at that time). This simple, but effective device, made seeding the cotton easier which created more of an opportunity to expand the sale of cotton. Before this invention, one slave could remove the seed from about a pound of short-staple cotton per day. This crude proto-type increased that amount to one hundred pounds a day. All of a sudden, what once was a small-profit crop became the future "King" of the

South. The textile mills of England and France could not buy enough. Everybody had to have their cotton.

THE FIRST COTTON GIN

Some forty years later, South Carolina's prominent Senator, John C. Calhoun, declared that slavery—far from being merely a "necessary evil"—was actually a "positive good." After the invention of the cotton gin in 1794 (patent date), the South had become incredibly wealthy (at least, some folks had), and the South began to provide more that 80% of ALL U.S. EXPORTS. Eli Whitney definitely put the South on the world map.

Along with all of this affluence and prosperity in the South, a Northern resentment began to grow. These two great sections of America were involved in completely separate economies with their own quirks, needs and motivations; they were definitely on different pages, as it were, and this will magnify over time.

Linking those two "Peoples" in some political bond was bound to end up in trouble.

UNDERSTANDING THE TIME

Before you get into the Civil War, you have to understand the times. Let's start with a bit of an analysis.

The War Between the States was not an isolated or single-issue affair. It was a slow-burn thru the early history of Colonial America that finally came to a head in late 1860. Keep in mind that we hadn't had our first centennial; we were still thinking as states (sovereign nations), not Americans. The brief time that we fought together against a common foe was fading into the past. People were becoming more local in their thinking once again. Kids forget the trials of their parents rather quickly.

I have always been one that believes that anthropology, sociology, geology and history go hand-in-hand. Simply put, what people do is determined, in part, by what they know and what they believe or perceive. Perception, to some folks, is reality, remember.

In 1860 America, our ancestors' ethics and moral behavior were not the same as ours by any stretch. A gentleman, for instance, would have been considered rude if he asked a woman a direct question. Women did not wear men's clothing... and same-sex marriages were never even considered an option. Can you imagine how a nineteenth century Abraham Lincoln would come across on a TV talk show? I would love to see the real Abraham Lincoln on *The View*.

What some people believe about Lincoln is more myth than fact, and what he really was would have everyone walking off the set. His male-chauvinist views and lack of real respect for the Negro Race would have had him nailed by our modern Press. He would have been run out of town on a rail. He was, by current standards, a Racist with a capital "R". Please keep in mind that Mr. Lincoln was not so much "pro-Negro" as he was "anti-slavery". The current movie "*Lincoln*" depicted him as a crusader of the Negro Race. The folks in Hollywood stated in their pre-press releases that "an army of historians have never found any instance of Lincoln being a bigot or racist". That's interesting in itself; I guess they haven't read the following:

From the 4th Lincoln/Douglas Debate, 1858: "I will say then that I am not, nor ever have been in favor of bringing about in anyway the social and political equality of the white and black races - that I am not nor ever have been in favor of making voters or jurors of negroes, nor of qualifying them to hold office, nor to intermarry with white people; and I will say in addition to this that there is a physical difference between the white and black races which I believe will forever forbid the two races living together on terms of social and political equality. And inasmuch as they cannot so live, while they do remain together there must be the position of superior and inferior, and I, as much as any other man, am in favor of having the superior position assigned to the white race. I say upon this occasion I do not perceive that because the white man is to have the superior position the negro (sic) should be denied everything." Abraham Lincoln

And, let's get this out front; this is what Old Abe said about slavery:

From Lincoln's Published Response to Horace Greeley, 1862: "My paramount object in this struggle is to save the Union, and is not either to save or to destroy slavery. If I could save the Union without freeing any slave I would do it, and if I could save it by freeing all the slaves I would do it; and if I could save it by freeing some and leaving others alone I would also do that. What I do about slavery and the colored race, I do because I believe it helps to save the Union; and what I forbear, I forbear because I do not believe it would help to save the Union. I shall do less whenever I shall believe what I am doing hurts the cause, and I shall do more whenever I shall believe doing more will help the cause."

Lincoln was obviously more of a "Unionist" and not an "Abolitionist." Am I missing anything here? Why isn't this clear?

Why, then, do we continue to promote untruths about this man? We, as a nation, have genuine heroes; we don't have to fabricate one. Let us, now, get your kids ready to understand the real Lincoln in his own time.... and to see the world as it was in 1860.

It is hard for their generation, one that drives thirty miles for a hamburger, to understand how isolated and regional we really were back then. Can you imagine your world without your cell phone and automobile? Communication was painfully slow in early America. It was unreliable, and was always open for malicious editing. What would keep anyone from sending false reports and slanted news in this time period? Where were the "Checks and Balances?" There were none.

As bad as "editorializing" has become in our modern world, can you imagine the rampant editing done in the powerful 19th century newspapers? That small, powerful force in society was instrumental in bringing this War on. All it takes in a modern report is the mere description of the forces at play; if you want the reader to like your guys, you refer to them as "freedom fighters". If you want your readers to hate the other guys, you refer to them as "terrorists". Now, insert the terms "slavers" and "righteous" in the press reports of the 19th century, and there you have it. This practice is as old as the Gutenberg Press of 1440.

We did not have a "National Frame of Mind" in 1860. People were born and lived their entire lives without traveling more than 25 miles from their place of birth; where were they going? Why were they going anywhere? How were they supposed to get there? Roads were still few and very crude. Not everyone owned a horse or a wagon, and it was dangerous to travel. One's safety was a constant concern. Most Americans were farmers in this time; they were tied down to their animals and their agrarian daily chores. Travel was a luxury for the rich, and a risk taken by need, only.

(Point of trivia: Wealthy people were known to have exhibited seashells in their front parlors during the 19th century. This little addition to their décor told visitors, without saying so, that they had enough money to travel to the ocean, and someone else could be paid to handle their domestic duties and obligations. Even in those days, "My tires are bigger than your tires." was still the thing, just applied differently.)

(Point of trivia: After the introduction of the interior gas lighting in the 19th century, some folks hung their prized "gasoliers" (a gas-fitted chandelier) above their dining tables. This would have said "money" to anyone who saw it; but, folks took it one step further, and placed an empty candelabra on the table indicating that: "We don't use candles anymore, we have gas.")

In 1860, a gentleman was not allowed to ask a female acquaintance a direct question. It would have been looked on as a blatant "faux pas" (pronounced "Fo Paw"... French word, means "serious gaff".) He would make a statement, and if she chose not to respond to the statement, the matter was dropped. It was during this period, by the way, that we were getting away from the social use of French. People began saying "Excuse my French." when they used a French term in polite conversation.

At the time of Mr. Lincoln, it was impolite to cross in front of a woman on a side walk; a woman was always allowed to enter the room ahead of the male and be served first in social gatherings.

This, then, becomes a real problem for modern-day historians to do their jobs. Because of the massive pressure from our current society's special interest groups, people who write or edit our public education's history books have to skirt real-life scenarios and morays. They tend to insert 21st century filters into their accounts, rendering the truth almost undetectable.

Modern-day feminists would have a hard time allowing a teacher to even infer such a behavior ever existed. Just by mentioning the fact that it happened causes some of these folks to insist that you were promoting it, instead of just passing the info along. It is the ploy of leaving something out... to shade the truth....to further their cause. I am not singling out feminists, either. There are a lot of groups that are going to have their feathers ruffled in this narrative. When you mess with the language, you mess with the truth; details count, especially in history.

Consider that the slang word for African-Americans has been edited out of Mark Twain's *Huckleberry Finn* in our school's libraries. Certainly, that word was used to describe minorities by

19th century contemporary writers. Removing words begins to skew the dynamics of that time, rendering the info "compromised" and false. "Political correctness" and "historical accuracy" cannot exist on the same plane; again, there is no room for politics in recording history.

If language, in itself, becomes the issue instead of the subject matter, then we all have to re-evaluate our roles in finding the truth. We either have to have an honest dialog, or just stay at home and watch another reality show.

American history has, indeed, been edited over time by succeeding generations; this is not a new development, just a more speeded up version. Mass communication can be a blessing or it can create havoc. Contemporary view-points dictated, and still do dictate the angle or "take" on events. The term "political correctness" describes the protocol of today's writers, of course, but it is not a new idea.

Ever since people began to record history---politics, religion, as well as local beliefs and superstitions, all played their parts on how something was chronicled. There has always been a type of "political correctness" in society. It went by different names, and was always in the background of all recorded materials; it just seems to be getting worse.

For one to understand just how we, as a nation, came to such bitter blows, we need to step back in time. The War Between the States did not just pop up one day, it simmered for a long time, as I said. There were a whole bunch of issues and a lot of distance between the groups that will play a part.

For those of my readers who saw our play, this will help you understand better the points that flew by during the show.

THE EARLY SETTLERS

America, before 1607, was a wide open and utterly undeveloped land. The Native Americans were concentrated mostly in the Eastern part of the continent, mostly because of the terrain and amiable climate. Large fertile areas, full of wild game, supported a bigger collection of peoples. The Indian nations were loosely organized and were always engaged in either trade or war depending on the local agreements or disagreements between neighboring tribes. What one has to stop to realize is that the introduction of the Europeans into this mix had several effects, some were good, and others were bad.

Current history books are being hard on that European arrival. If you were to believe these contemporaries, Europeans caused nothing but death and destruction, and ruined a pristine environment. Let us ignore the vast nation that they produced, full of research, opportunity and the most advanced civilization ever. Those that believe that we have ruined this great land are the same ones sitting with their IPODs, collecting their parent's money, and blogging their gripes while using the internet. Some folks simply have no real common sense. If these "enlightened few" were true to their beliefs, they would be drinking water from a mosquito-infested pond, and sending smoke signals to their friends on the next hill. Realistically, that would be where their technology would still be. Good luck with the malaria, dudes. These folks used to be called "hippies" back in the 60s.

Welcome, then, to our first confrontation, and our first bit of reconstruction of fact.

THE NATIVE AMERICANS

The Native Americans "gave as good as they got", as best they could, in any event. If one were to believe modern writers, the Native Americans were a peaceful, nature-centered group who just wanted to left alone. (Let's all go see *Pocahontas* one more time.) Native Americans are portrayed as loving, kind naturists who gathered fruits and nuts and communed with squirrels.

Reality check: The 17th and 18th Century Native Americans were a carnivorous, aggressive people who had to be that way in order to survive. Nowhere in any research that I can muster, is it even implied that Native Americans were vegans. (A "Vegan" is a vegetarian on steroids, basically.)

They used fire to clear areas as well as to drive animals to slaughter. They were not members of PETA or the Sierra Club.

They were outright brutal to their game. These people tolerated no guff from neighboring tribes. They were like all human beings with limited skills and tools; they made do with what they could improvise. They were always looking for a "bigger bow".

Their method, for instance, for killing buffalo is an example: they would set fire to the plains grasses to scare the herds over a cliff and then watch them smash themselves on the rocks below. Buffalo calves were killed along with the others in the same way. (Little, tiny, sweet buffalo-ettes were crunched right alongside Momma and Daddy.) Native Americans were a resourceful, energetic and determined group; you bet. How long do you think a real vegan today would last alone on the plains?

Native Americans were, and still are, real human beings; they did what everyone else did. Life is life, people are people. Survival is all that mattered. They are not a magical group... just people.

The truth be told, little Pocahontas and Captain Smith never were romantically involved; he was already a married man with a wife back in England, and Pocahontas was close to twelve years old. These two never had any kind of relationship beyond the empathy that a little girl showed to the plight of another human in need of help. (She did, however marry another member of that settlement.) How many little girls have grown up with that harmless, but deceptive twist in historical fact? I must, again, point out that History and Hollywood have little in common.

Were these Natives really all that peaceful? If that had been the case, they wouldn't have already had war-clubs and battle-axes when the Whites set foot on this continent; these weapons were not created in response to an invasion. Native Americans were always beating the snot out of each other, taking each other slaves, and trying to move into the other tribe's hunting grounds. Testosterone comes in all colors, folks. "War" is a human condition, not a "European concept". Why, then, blame the Europeans for a general human condition?

Anyone that will defend the current interpretation of Native Americans before the Europeans got here should spend an evening at a local Indian council meeting in New Mexico. These folks are folks. They had jealousies and quarrels just like their contemporaries still do. They argued, fought, and cussed. I lived in New Mexico for years; I have seen these things happen. Watch TV in Albuquerque long enough, and catch the Tribal coverage. These folks can still swing a mean battle-axe.

Does anybody remember the story of the Lost Colony of Roanoke in North Carolina? That colony "disappeared" in 1587... and most scholars agree that they were either wiped out or moved in with local tribes. No one knows for sure what happened to them.

Keep in mind, that I don't fault the Indians for this; they were doing what most people would do when threatened by invaders. They would not have been human to have reacted in any other way.

I enjoy bantering with the Native Americans that I get to meet. They have a gentle sense of humor, and serve a tasty dog dish. (Although Federal Law prohibits the sale of dog meat, Indian Reservations still are allowed to partake, and they still have some restaurants on the reservations that serve up a side of "Spot".) I am not making this up. Every culture has its tastes.

We also have to put aside the "Blame Game" in this narrative to accomplish anything. The facts are what they are: Europeans introduced mumps, syphilis, measles and host of European maladies; the Native Americans got them back with their tobacco. Any time cultures collide, interesting things happen.

According to recent statistics, more that 440,000 Americans die each year from tobacco-related cancer. Marijuana, peyote, and squash were also good paybacks. (I hate squash.) There is enough human nature in all of us. Come on, boys and girls, Indians are people, too. Let's give them a hug.

Let us now get serious about the opening up of our nation, shall we? No more goofy meandering around the subject.

It is important that the reader understands the details of our Colonial History. It all ties in. Take the time to really become an expert in this area. Once you have a firm understanding of the 1700s, then you will really enjoy the 1800s.

To practice a little early American reality, start by eating the way our ancestors did. The English ate with both hands and still do. The forks used by the settlers in Jamestown had two prongs. (The fork is the evolution of the dagger.) The knives were broad and had a curve; knives were used to scoop with as well as cut with. Our ancestors ate with the fork in the left hand, and the knife in the right. They only laid their knives down to pick up something else. We ate like this for 300 years in America.

A serviette (table napkin) was used by everyone to protect their hand-made clothes; men tucked, ladies pinned.

By the mid-19th century, forks were set to the left of the plate, spoons on the right, and the broad knife at the top of the plate.

(Point of trivia: We toured the Rowan House in Bardstown, Kentucky a few years past, and their tour-guide told everyone that we didn't have knives in 1858. If we needed something cut, we had our servants cut it in the kitchen. You really have to be careful when you go to these historical sites; they are filled with a lot of the inaccurate information. I loved those zippers on the backs of their antebellum dresses.)

COLONIAL AMERICA

The Colonial history of the United States covers the European settlements from the start of colonization of America until their incorporation into the United States. We will do this step by step. The reader is allowed to read this next part a few times until it really sinks in. If you do, you will understand more of what happens later. Take your time, this is for fun; there will be no written test. (Now is the time to get your coffee.)

In the late 16th century, (that means in the 1500s), England, France, Spain and the Netherlands started major colonization programs in eastern North America. They knew there was gold, timber, furs and other good stuff to be had. Europe, by this time, had depleted most of its virgin timber and the wildlife had been almost completely consumed. Everything was free for the taking in this new world, sort of.

It was the adventurers, soldiers, farmers, and tradesmen that took the challenge first. They were our first real entrepreneurs; God Bless them.

"Diversity" is not a new concept; it was a real American characteristic from the start. It was the Dutch of New Netherland, the Swedes and Finns of New Sweden, the English Quakers of Pennsylvania, the English Puritans of New England, and the English settlers of Jamestown that came along with the "worthy poor" of Georgia. These folks came to the new continent and built colonies with distinctive social, religious, political and economic styles. The definition of an "American" was born defining itself as a "mixed puppy".

The introduction of African labor began in 1619. That group contributed to this mix and their population grew to around

37

75,000 by 1739.

In 1739, the first violent uprising by the slaves happened in South Carolina. As more and more slaves were brought into this new country, more agitations and minor revolts occurred. This lead to a mass hanging of fifty slaves. This "over-kill" was done to set an example of the hard rule by their owners. This illustrates how increased numbers of different ethnic cultures, when forced together, create a lot of friction.

You would think that someone in a university "study" could conclude that all of the mandates and laws that forced people together over the past 250 years have been the real source of upheaval. People merge in their own time, always have.

Let us now look back at a critical turn in local politics, American Colony-Style.

CHAPTER TWO

THE FRENCH AND INDIAN WAR

In 1651, while Cromwell was master of England, the first of the famous Navigation Acts was passed to contain and promote English control over colonial commerce and trade. The heavy hand of the Mother country was about to begin. The Act's major provisions stated that all goods grown or manufactured in Asia, Africa, or America should be transported to England only in English vessels. It also stated that the goods of any European country imported into England must be brought in by British vessels, or in vessels of the country producing them. Things began to simmer as English rule began to become local. (Remember the old adage… "all politics are local.")

As the young colonies were being developed, the French, as well as various Native tribes, were attempting to hold onto or grab what they could get. Time was of the essence to all of those involved; territories were opened, protected, fought over, and changed hands. The inevitable finally occurred in 1754.

The French and Indian War started over land disputes in the Ohio River Valley. This war was fought between Great Britain and its two greatest enemies, the French and the Indians of North America. Most of the battles were in Canada. American colonists, including George Washington, fought with the British in this war, which lasted from 1754 to 1763. The British won the war and won the right to keep Canada and several other possessions in the New World. "The French and Indian War," also known as "The Seven Years War" ended with the Treaty of Paris in 1763.

During the "Period of Neglect", as it was also referred to, England had little time to baby-sit their American colonies. The French and Indian War exhausted England's reserves and its diplomatic energies. This conflict had distracted England with a near-global scope, and it was only after the Treaty was signed in Paris, that Mother England had time to go back to see to her distant children, the American Colonies. By the time she could focus on the colonies, they had matured somewhat, and were used to the new freedoms of self-control that had developed. They were not the same bunch of English settlers that had initially landed in the New World. These folks had begun to take root and felt like they had earned some new respect for their efforts.

It was at this time that the British government began to demand that the colonies pay their fair share of government and military costs. The French and Indian War had cost King George III a lot of money, and he wanted it back. King George felt fully justified that the Colonies had to pay for all of the protection that his armies had provided during these seven years; taxes were then demanded.

KING GEORGE III

The colonists were not too keen on giving chunks of money to the mother country for a job that they thought was less than effective. Not long before, for instance, England had slipped up badly and allowed Pontiac, the Ottawa Chief, to slip by into the settlements and kill several thousand people. The same settlers were also banking on the opening up of new territory which would allow them to prosper even more with the vast raw materials and wild game. The English government had issued a "Proclamation of 1763" that restrained the colonists from moving westward. This proclamation was viewed as a complete denial of their rights. The colonists could not understand the limitations. They wanted a piece of the new action, plain and simple. They had tasted a bit of wealth, and they were not going to just let it go.

1764

In 1764, the English added to the Navigation Act which had controlled commerce since 1760. This new infringement on the already agitated colonial merchants was "The Revenue Act of 1764", better known as "The Sugar Act". This unwanted and nuisance of a tax put a three-cent tax on foreign refined sugar and increased taxes on coffee, indigo, and certain kinds of wine; it also banned the importation of rum and French wines. These taxes affected only a certain part of the population, but the affected merchants were very vocal.

The taxes were raised without the consent of the colonists. This was one of the first instances in which colonists wanted a have a say in how much they were taxed. This time period has been described as "The Eve of Revolution".

This act also expanded the jurisdiction of the vice-admiralty courts and was aimed to curb smuggling. Smuggling was a major portion of the total colonial commerce. The colonists protested again, and called for less control by England, and more say in their local matters. King George turned a deaf ear.

1765

On November 1, 1765, The Stamp Act required legal documents, (including newspapers, legal papers, land contracts, marriage licenses), to bear revenue stamps purchased from Royal stamp distributors. Lawyers and newspaper men in the colonies began openly proclaiming their resentment. Tempers were flaring over this additional intrusion into colonial commerce and a growing number of colonists began to sympathize.

A Boston group calling itself "Sons of Liberty" got into the fray and burned the local stamp distributor in effigy.

Panic ensued, of course, among Stamp distributors in almost every American port. They began to resign because they were not about to die for an English law that threatened their homes and families. With no one to sell the revenue stamps, the whole idea was abandoned by London. On March 18, 1766, the Stamp Act was repealed.

This was a taste of liberation for the colonials and it gave them more encouragement and resolve. The other guy had blinked, and the Colonists knew it.

In the same year, 1765, Parliament approved "The Quartering Act of 1765". This required colonists to house British troops and to feed them. This was illegal in England. The colonials began to feel less and less equal to their cousins in England, and more like the ugly step-child who is forced to eat out on the back stoop. Not only were the colonists ticked off by the order, they had to deal with a bunch of ill-mannered, aggressive, young males living in their homes. Imagine all of your rowdy son's friends moving into your house, completely uncontrolled and absolutely arrogant as well as stupid. This was not an easy thing, to say the least. Making the whole matter worse, a lot of well-protected young women were now thrust into socially uncomfortable circumstances. Just imagine, if you will, five young males living a few feet from your sixteen year old daughter. That will keep you up for a few nights.

1766

On the same day it repealed the Stamp Act, the English Parliament passed the "Declaratory Act". This little law stated that the British government had total power to legislate any laws governing the American colonies in all cases whatsoever. They had effectively let the colonies know that there would be no real local law.

This was probably the straw that broke the camel's back for a lot of already aggravated colonials. The ensuing moves by England just proceeded to nail the coffin lid shut, as far as a lot of colonials were concerned. The local boys were about to play hard ball with their English King.

1767

The English Parliament passed the "Townshend Revenue Act" to offset the cost of administering and protecting the American settlers. Items taxed included imports such as tea, glass, paper, lead and paint. The Act also established a colonial board of customs commissioners in Boston.

In October of that same year, Bostonians decided to reinstate a boycott against English luxury items. English merchants began to grumble that England needed a heavier hand in the colonies. Pressure was mounting on both sides of the Atlantic.

1770

England sent more troops to the colonies; a bigger show of force. More resentment was felt...and things were at a flash-point.

THE BOSTON MASSACRE

In March of 1770, about fifty citizens got into a beef with a British sentinel and his officer. Tempers flared, support was called in, snow-balls and rocks were thrown. The soldiers, fearing for their lives, fired into the crowd. Three died by the shots, two later died from their wounds. A trial was held later, and the soldiers were found guilty of man-slaughter.

This occurrence led the Governor to evacuate the troops from Boston. The colonists saw another "blink" from London.

We were getting closer to armed revolt. The Boston Massacre had left 5 dead and opened the way for pro-separatist writers to flourish.

Pressured from the reaction to the taxes on luxury items, Parliament retracts the taxes on everything but tea. King George would have it no other way.

In a slightly covert way, Parliament makes an agreement with the East India Company and offers the colonies a carrot, so to speak. If the colonies were to buy all of their tea from The East India Tea Company, they could get a lower price. The hook: the colonies were going to still have to pay the tax on the tea. The bottom line was that the colonial tea merchants still got a better deal on the price, even figuring in the tax, but they would be allowing Parliament the right to tax them. The colonies still had no representation in Parliament. The colonials saw thru the game and balked. They were not going to pay any tax unless they had a vote on matters in Parliament. These colonists knew the game.

When the first shipments of tea were sent to the Colonies, trouble erupted first in Charleston. The cargo was detained and placed in a private warehouse. The tax was not going to be paid, period. (Three years later, it was sold to help finance the War.)

When the three ships entered Boston harbor, more trouble came quickly. These three ships, *The Beaver, The Dartmouth,* and *The Eleanor* had a total of three hundred and thirty-two cases of black, Chinese, loose-leaf tea on board.

Prior to their arrival, protesters in three other colonies had earlier successfully prevented the unloading of taxed tea and these Bostonians were not about to have it any other way. Tensions grew, negotiations got threatening, and The Royal Governor, Thomas Hutchinson, refused to bend to the protestors' demands. The stand-off was getting more and more complicated and dangerous.

THE BOSTON TEA PARTY

The arrival of three tea ships ignited a furious reaction from the citizenry. The crisis came to a climax on December 16, 1773, when almost 7,000 ticked- off Bostonians assembled about the wharf. You could cut the tension with a knife; these folks were ready to make something happen, whatever it was.

Earlier, at a mass meeting at the Old South Meeting House, it had been resolved that the tea ships should just leave the harbor without payment of any duty.

A small committee was selected to take this message to the Customs House to force the release of the ships out of the harbor. The frustrated Collector of Customs refused to allow the ships to leave without payment of the duty; it was a stalemate.

The committee reported back to the mass meeting and a series of cat-calls and "boos" filled the meeting hall. It was now early evening and a group of about 200 men, some disguised as Mohawk Indians, assembled on a near-by hill. The men separated into three groups and began whooping Indian war chants as they marched "two-by-two" to the wharf. They descended upon the three ships, forced the captains to relinquish the keys to the lockers, and proceeded to dump the tea into the harbor.

The accounts vary on the number of participants that dressed up like Mohawk Indians and got on board the ships; from fifty to two hundred. Samuel Adams organized about sixty members of "The Sons of Liberty" to spearhead the move. All totaled, about $18,000 worth of tea was destroyed.

SAMUEL ADAMS

Interestingly enough, court testimony later revealed that the "Indians" did no damage to the ships, (they had no problem with the ship's owners), and actually swept the decks clean before they left. They were very neat.

The East India Company's losses, caused by the Boston Tea Party, created a deep wound. Here, in this act of vandalism, a group of white men dressed as Indians, dumped three shiploads of tea into the Boston harbor in an orchestrated and illegal protest of all tariffs on tea imports. Such an act angered the British who closed the New England's most important harbor. Boston was going to pay for this assault on English sovereignty.

1774

Parliament hit the roof. Angered members of Parliament responded in 1774 with the "Coercive Acts", or "Intolerable Acts". Among other provisions, these Acts put an end to local self-government in Massachusetts. With this new act, a new version of the 1765 Quartering Act was enacted by the English Parliament to provide housing for the British troops in occupied houses and taverns. Husbands, again, worried for their wives' and daughters' safety, and, again for good reason. The British soldiers helped themselves to the ample opportunities. They grew bolder, too.

Colonists, up and down the Thirteen Colonies, in turn, responded to the Coercive Acts with additional acts of protest. The province of Massachusetts Bay was in a state of crisis following the passage. They formed the "extra-legal"

Massachusetts Provincial Congress and began organizing militia units independent of British control.

THE FIRST CONTINENTAL CONGRESS

In September of 1774, The First Continental Congress was called to order in Philadelphia, Pennsylvania. It was at this gathering that the members hammered out a letter to King George asking him to be gracious enough to repeal the acts and to stop the coordinated resistance against them. A total of 56 delegates, representing every colony, except Georgia, came together and agreed, on September 17, to formerly oppose the Coercive Acts. This spirit was sweeping the colonies; there was something in the air.

A silversmith and organizer for the "cause", Paul Revere, headed out of Boston to rally support from New York and Philadelphia. Before he could get his story out, his buddies had jumped ahead of him, and members of "The Sons of Liberty" had begun to stir the pot and make it happen. The boys in the Massachusetts legislature added their voices in June. Delegates were chosen in all the colonies except Georgia, and they met in Carpenter's Hall in Philadelphia.

Great and influential leaders such as Washington, Lee, and Henry of Virginia; Dickinson of Pennsylvania; Samuel and John Adams of Massachusetts; and Roger Sherman of Connecticut, all made the trip and had a boatload of ideas... and the courage to make it happen.

This Congress was not a constitutional body; many of its members had been chosen irregularly. Its authority was limited to the willingness of the people to respect and obey its suggestions and mandates. The very fact that it had become a reality was an idea that King George could not or did not want to fully comprehend. He was, as we say in the South, "a slow leak" in matters of abstract thinking. These boys in Philadelphia attempted no national legislation and it was controlled by members with cool heads and solid reasoning. These men were not all "fireballs"... they were grounded men of reason and respect; they were English gentlemen with American tempering.

They made their first move by making a mild declaration of rights. They made it clear to King George that they had no ideas of independence... but... they left the option hanging open.

Some of these men were loyal to England and wanted no more than their "just rights" from their mother country. Others had had enough and wanted an end to the ties. Before all was said and done, this congress also approved the policy of "non-intercourse" with Great Britain, and formed an association to carry it out. The forming of this association, which, at first, constituted the revolutionary machinery, was an act of great importance.

Its objective was to secure a redress of grievances by peaceful methods, by enforcing the non-importation and non-consumption agreement. To carry out this purpose, committees were to be formed in every county or township in the colonies. These worked under the guidance of the Committees of Correspondence. The local committees targeted every loyalist who refused to comply with the recommendations of the Congress. The loyalists made a feeble effort at a counter organization, but the patriots were so furious in their opposition that little came of it. Not until the next year, in 1775, did the patriots begin to form associations pledged to oppose the aggressions of the King by force of arms.

This effort was monumental and troubling because of the continued loyalty among some of its members to the Throne. Not everyone wanted to cause any trouble with England, nor did they want to entertain the idea of separating from her. To some members, King George was still their King, and they were still very English. This inner turmoil among the American colonists at that Congress was a difficult tight-rope to walk, to say the least; the elusive question was how to handle this crisis.

King George III was a man used to having his own way and was not going to be pushed about by his subjects. The crisis escalated, and an increasing number of the colonists were not going to be denied their cause… the American Revolutionary War was to kick off near Boston later in 1775.

1775

February 9, 1775: The English Parliament declared Massachusetts to be in a "state of rebellion."

March 23, 1775: Virginian Patrick Henry delivered his speech against the British rule stating: "Give me liberty or give me death!"

PATRICK HENRY

APRIL 1775

Massachusetts Governor Gage was ordered to enforce the Coercive Acts and suppress "open rebellion" among the colonists by all necessary force. King George chose not to send anyone to the colonies to calm things down or to even listen to the grievances. The story, later, was that he failed to do so because he was sick. Regardless, this lack of diplomacy, in its simplest form, might have averted a greater problem.

A Provincial Congress was held in Cambridge, Massachusetts during which John Hancock and Joseph Warren began defensive preparations for a state of war.

CHAPTER THREE

THE REVOLUTIONARY WAR

The Boston Tea Party and the recurring problems finally came to a head.

By April of 1775, King George decided that he was going to put a stop to all of the treason and mischief that had been brewing in his American Colonies.

Looking back, it had been a sad day in the course of English politics when George III rose to power. England had had almost two hundred years of easy sailing and little trouble with their monarchs when George III used the rising Tory Party as a catapult to do what his momma had kept hounding him to do... "Be a King, George!"

Historians agree that King George was a man of limited intellect and did not have what it took to be a great or inspiring leader. None the less, the boy was King, and that trumps "smart" in any time period. He was petty in his dealings with his subjects, bestowing rewards on those that played up to him, and acted childishly toward those of character and good sense that would not cater to his every whim. He was downright nasty to them, to be truthful.

King George rid himself of all decent and honorable advisors and replaced them with, among others, Lord North, his pick for the new Prime Minister.

North was amiable and had some economic skills to note, but was merely a puppet for George to string along. The combination of the two at this time of rebellion was a recipe for disaster.

George III was vindictive and would have revenge against the colonies at all costs. He ended up losing England's finest jewel in her Imperial crown, the American Colonies, because of it.

After hearing of the assault on his pride in Boston, George III was fit to be tied. England, as a whole, stood aghast at the impudence of her sometime submissive colonists. The irate King, with monumental pigheadedness and inability to discern the signs of the times, resolved to humble the Americans once for all. This old boy thought that he could pull this off without a sweat, and did not doubt for a moment that his will was all he needed.

King George wrote, (of the colonist), "They will be lions while we are lambs: but if we take the resolute part, they will undoubtedly prove very meek."

King George now led his Parliament to pass four drastic measures against the people of Massachusetts.

First: The Boston Port Bill, which removed the capital from Boston to Salem, and closed the port of Boston to the commerce of the world.

Second: The Regulating Act, which annulled the Massachusetts Charter and transformed the colony to an absolute despotism.

Third: An Act providing that persons accused of certain crimes in connection with riots be transported to England, or to some place outside of the colony for trial.

Fourth: Made it legal to quarter troops in any town in Massachusetts.

These were soon followed by the Quebec Act, which extended the province of Quebec to include all the territory west of the Alleghenies and north of the Ohio River to the Mississippi -- except what had been granted by Royal Charter. It is supposed that the act was intended to prevent pioneers from settling in the Ohio country, and to win the favor of the French Catholics.

Two years before these acts were passed, in 1772, Massachusetts, led by Samuel Adams, had made an important move toward concerted action. "Committees of Correspondence" had been appointed in every town in the colony for the purpose of guarding the interests of liberty. The next year, Virginia suggested the forming of a permanent "Committee of Correspondence" to extend to all the colonies. This was gradually done, and the system was very effective in spreading the doctrine of resistance. The boys in the colonies had foreseen the possibility of further tyranny, and were one step ahead of George.

To counter the drastic British measures, Massachusetts now made an appeal for aid, and through these committees, the people were prepared for an immediate response. From Maine to Georgia, they made common cause with their brethren of the Bay Colony, and South Carolina sounded the keynote in these ringing words, "The whole country must be animated with one great soul, and all Americans must stand by one another, even unto death."

George Washington offered to arm and equip a thousand men at his own expense and to lead them to the relief of Boston. Thomas Jefferson set forth the view in a pamphlet called the "Summary View," that Parliament had no right or any authority whatever in the colonies. This was, in effect, an absolute statement of treason.

Nearly all the colonies joined in an agreement of non-intercourse with England. As the day approached for the Port Bill to take effect, shipments of cattle, grain, and produce from the other colonies began to pour into Boston. The day finally came, and throughout the country, it was generally kept as a day of fasting and prayer; the church bells were tolled, and flags were put at half-mast on the ships in the harbors. Had the English king been able to glance over to America on that day, he would have abandoned every thought of punishing a single colony without having to deal with all of them; he would have seen that but two courses lay before him -- to recede from his position, or to make war upon a continent. My Grandfather would have said, "King George had his eye on the taxi coming from his left, so to speak, while the bus was about to nail him from his right." Again, "King" trumps "smart"....and England was about to pay for this bitter truth.

King George has to take total blame for the War. It was his sole decision to keep the tax on the tea and he would not budge on letting his colonies have any involvement that they had demanded as loyal English subjects. Had he negotiated, or had anyone around him that he would allow to speak freely about the situation, we may well have still been part of the United Kingdom.

Dr. Joseph Warren, of Massachusetts, drew up a forceful challenge to King George's hold on the colonies with a set of resolutions that stated that any king who violates the chartered rights of the people forfeits their allegiance.

This document also stated that the Regulating Act was null and void. Massachusetts, in that spirit, set up a Provisional Government of its own.

King George had just been slapped publicly, metaphorically speaking.

PROHIBITORY ACT OF 1775

THE FUSE IS LIT

In late 1775, the Parliament of Great Britain, under Lord North, First Lord of the Treasury, decided that sterner measures would be taken to subdue the rebellion now underway in the 13

American colonies. England decreed a blockade against the trade of the American colonists. "... all manner of trade and commerce" would be prohibited, and any ship that was found trading "shall be forfeited to his Majesty, as if the same were the ships and effects of open enemies." The goal of the Act was to destroy the American economy by making it incapable of operating by means of prohibiting trade with any country. The colonies were either going to be choked to death... or come out fighting. This was it, folks; we were going to war.

This First Continental Congress sat for about seven weeks and then was adjourned. They decided to reconvene the next 10th of May; King George got their first communication later that year on October 26.

One of the members of Parliament remarked at that time, "When your lordships look at the papers transmitted us from America -- when you consider their decency, firmness, and wisdom, you cannot but respect their cause. . . . For myself, I must declare and avow, that in all my reading and observation . . . that for solidity of reasoning, force of sagacity, and wisdom of conclusion . . . no nation or body of men can stand in preference to the Congress at Philadelphia. I trust that it is obvious to your lordships, that all attempts to impose servitude upon such men, to establish despotism over such a mighty continental nation must be vain, must be fatal." The old boy could see the bus that George couldn't.

Back in Massachusetts, the summer of 1775 had been one of accelerated excitement. The people of Massachusetts had scurried about and worked out ways to stop the Regulation Act from happening. They surrounded the courthouses and forced the King's officers to resign; they refused to serve as jurymen; they met for military drill on the village green of every town.

Numerous other leaders, including John Hancock and Dr. Joseph Warren, helped organize and orchestrate the defiance; John Adams and Samuel Adams kept busy as well.

General Gage had returned to Massachusetts with an army; his intention was to frighten the colonists by offering them a look at British bayonets. He had recently been made the "Civil" as well as "Military Governor", and was making it known. The colonists countered the bravado by organizing into bands of "minutemen". This new militia was to be called out in a minute's notice.

Gage sent a party of soldiers to seize some powder at Charles Town (an area of Boston); the rumor spread that they had fired on the citizens, and in less than two days, twenty thousand farmers were under arms, marching toward Boston. The rumor proved false, and they returned to their homes.

Late in October, a Provincial Congress met at Concord, with John Hancock as President, and Joseph Warren the Chairman of a committee appointed to collect military stores. This Congress dissolved in December, and another met at Cambridge in February and proceeded to organize the militia and to appoint officers.

During the winter and spring of 1775, the tensions continued to increase, and everything looked more and more like war was the end result. King George and Parliament, as well as Gage, had miscalculated when they believed that the presence of an army would awe the colonists. They were completely wrong about changing the colonists from roaring lions into fawning lambs.

The colonists were better prepared than King George had even considered. They were fit, hardened farmers, capable of rigorous activities and skilled in weapons. They were strong and they knew it. Their bodies had been developed in clearing away the forest, in tilling the soil, in fishing and shipbuilding; they had become expert marksmen in fighting Indians and hunting wild animals. Many of them had gained an excellent military training in the late war with France. They also knew their adversaries.

Gage issued a proclamation offering full pardon to everyone except Samuel Adams and John Hancock. It was an offer that fell on deaf ears. These newly energized colonists were not going to heed any threats from their English cousins. They only kept on organizing, drilling, and collecting military stores in the towns.

Gage had been ordered to arrest Adams and Hancock, who had been elected to the Second Continental Congress. He was to capture and send these two trouble makers to England for trial.

The two patriot leaders, fearing arrest, had slipped away to Lexington. The British General had discovered their hiding place, and, on the night of the 18th of April, sent a body of eight hundred regulars to make the arrest. He also intended to seek out and destroy the stores of powder and shot and anything else he could ferret out in Concord.

Deep in the darkness of the night, the troops rowed across the Charles River, and, by midnight, they were well on the way to Lexington. Every precaution for secrecy had been taken, but the colonial spies had been alerted, and had uncovered the operation. The warning spread quickly through the night.

THE RIDE

I suppose most of us have heard about that famous ride of Paul Revere.

Like most stories told and re-told, it has become a little out of whack, as well. Let us have a bit of recess at this point to really see what happened. Here is the story.

The poem by Henry Wadsworth Longfellow, *"The Midnight Ride of Paul Revere"*, sets us up for a lot of myths.

Nowhere in that poem does Longfellow actually say that Paul Revere yelled "The British are coming!", yet, that is what people will swear he said. Quotes that never happened cause a lot of goofy and inaccurate history. Read it again, if you want to. I have read it several times of late, and I tell you... it is not in there. Most accounts written in that time indicate that he warned everyone that the "Regulars are out... the regulars are out... "... and so they were; close to 800 heavily armed British Regulars, and they were looking for trouble. The second big goof by Longfellow was that Paul was waiting to see signals that were to be sent to him, when he ACTUALLY had them placed in the Church in Boston to alert the boys ACROSS the RIVER. (There was no "SEA".)

TO CONTINUE

As the colonists continued to organize, arm, and form militias, the British military hoped to nip the revolution in the bud by sweeping into Massachusetts and other areas to scatter the growing make-shift armies of the colonists. The colonists were expecting the invasion and had laid careful plans to give as much advance warning as they could to their forces in the smaller towns and countryside.

Dr. Joseph Warren had made elaborate plans for a system of informants and riders who could quickly warn the colonists at a moment's notice. There were dozens of un-named volunteers that rode that night, but, over time, their names got lost. The three riders of note were Paul Revere, Dr. Samuel Prescott, and William Dawes.

PAUL REVERE

Paul Revere was a well-known master goldsmith, silversmith, engraver, and watchmaker. He was also a devoted member of The Sons of Liberty, and used his skills as an engraver to create inflammatory political cartoons that were used to bring the message out into the hands of hundreds.

His version of the Boston Massacre was very influential in spurring this conflict into happening.

ENGRAVING OF BOSTON MASSACRE BY PAUL REVERE

THE BOSTON MASSACRE

(The Boston Massacre was the killing of five colonists by British regulars on March 5, 1770. It was the culmination of tensions in the American colonies that had been growing since Royal troops first appeared in Massachusetts in October of 1768 to enforce the heavy tax burden imposed by the Townshend Acts.)

In 1774, and the Spring of 1775, Paul Revere was employed by the Boston Committee of Correspondence and the Massachusetts Committee of Safety as an express rider to carry news, messages, and copies of resolutions as far away as New York and Philadelphia. He took the job as courier because he needed the money. The fact that many of these new sanctions were killing his business spurred him on for several reasons. The English blockade on Boston was killing most businesses, and he really believed that there had to be some action taken.

At an earlier meeting with members of The Sons of Liberty in Charles Town, Paul Revere had arranged with three men to place a signal in the old North Church for the direction of movement by the Regulars; one lantern, if they were marching by land, (out Boston Neck), two lanterns, if they took the water route across the Charles River, (again, there was no "sea," except in Longfellow's mind). The lanterns were to be placed in the belfry by Robert Newman for less than a minute, which was long enough to be seen by The Sons of Liberty across the river and, unfortunately, by the British Regulars.

Dr. Joseph Warren instructed Revere to ride to Lexington and warn Samuel Adams and John Hancock that British troops were marching to arrest them.

After being rowed across the Charles River to Charles Town by two associates, Revere verified that the local "Sons of Liberty" committee had seen his pre-arranged signals, borrowed a horse from a friend, Deacon John Larkin, and began the famous ride.

On the way to Lexington, Revere "alarmed" the country-side, stopping at each house, and arrived in Lexington about midnight. As he approached the house of Reverend Jonas Clark, where Adams and Hancock were staying, a sentry asked that he not make so much noise. "Noise!" cried Revere, "You'll have noise enough before long. The regulars are coming out!"

After delivering his message, Revere was joined by a second rider, William Dawes, who had been sent on the same errand by a different route.

Dawes' route was west and north, a longer route; it helped make sure the message got thru the British Army road-blocks. Presscott later joined them outside of Lexington.

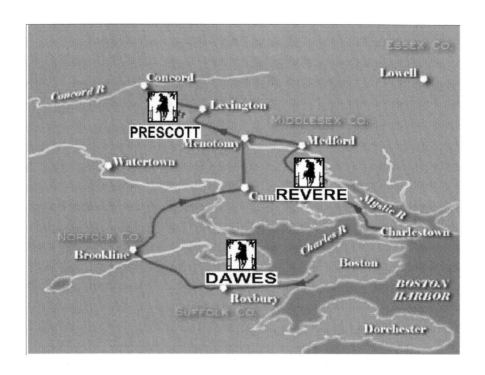

MAP OF THE THE RIDE

After deciding to continue on to Concord where weapons and supplies were hidden, Revere and Dawes were joined by a third rider, Dr. Samuel Prescott, a young physician. Soon after, all three were arrested by a British patrol. Prescott escaped almost immediately, and Dawes soon after.

Revere was held for some time and then released. Left without a horse, Revere returned to Lexington in time to witness part of the battle on the Lexington Green.

On the way to Concord, the British chased Dawes into the yard of a local farmhouse; here, Dawes pulled a clever ruse that allowed him to avoid capture. When he entered the yard of the farmstead, he shouted that he had "lured two British officers in." This made his pursuers think an ambush had been prepared, giving time for Dawes to escape a bit later on foot.

Samuel Prescott was not so lucky either. He was captured, but, like Dawes, he used trickery and evasive tactics to outwit the British. Prescott was the only one of the three to make it to his ultimate destination, Concord.

My revolutionary hero is Samuel Prescott. (There is no image of this hero that I can find, sorry.) He finished the midnight ride and told the whole village of Concord the British Regulars were coming to confiscate their weapons.

Because Dawes had been captured along with Revere, they did not finish the trip to Concord. Dawes escaped on foot, but ended up lost in the wilderness. Revere had his horse taken from him, leaving him stranded in Lexington. Had Prescott not finished the ride to Concord, those military stores would have certainly been captured and the colonial militia would have been unable to continue the fight....the Battle of Concord would have never happened, and the British Army would have never been as badly beaten early on as they were.

Samuel Prescott was captured early in the conflict and taken prisoner near Fort Ticonderoga. At the age of 26, Prescott died at in a nasty British prison in Halifax, Nova Scotia. He was a true American hero.

The Revolutionary War began at Lexington on April 19, 1775. After years of hardship, heartbreak, and thousands of lives lost, we finally achieved victory when General Cornwallis surrendered his army at Yorktown in 1781. That act effectively ended the war and the colonies were free of their English King. It was time to get a new form of government up and running. Cornwallis's sword had been accepted by General Benjamin Lincoln while a British band played "The World Turned Upside Down". This had been the last major battle of the war, although some minor skirmishes took place for the next two years. The Treaty of Paris ended the war in 1783. We, as a nation, were blessed to have real men of breeding and honor at just the right time.

Too many revolutions have happened thru time just to end up leaving the people with a worse government or some horrible dictator. Remember Cuba? Everyone couldn't wait to get rid of Batista... and guess what they ended up with... you got it, Fidel Castro.

As a side note, despite stories told, George Washington was never really offered the crown directly. The rumor of that story surfaces in the 1820s, and is an elaboration of some words from a friend of Washington in a letter. Nice story, but not true.

George Washington did, however, turn down the offer by Congress to be President for life; he served two terms.

Because of this kind of selfless leadership, we, as a nation, had a firm foundation to build on. That is not to say that all of our founding fathers were saints, there is always one or two in every crowd, so to speak. We were in good hands back then.

UNDERSTANDING THE TIME, PART TWO

Here is where we get down to the early issues that will lead us to war less than eighty years later. This is important stuff. Take your time; no need to rush.

The divide between Americans in this country was not only cultural, but physical. Today, we travel ten miles to the football game or twenty miles to see our kin. Those distances don't matter today, but, consider this: figure a man walks around three miles an hour; a man on foot, in good weather, level terrain, no hostiles, can walk 30 miles in a day, 40 if he pushes it. Travel by wagon, using horses or mules, would get you from fifteen to twenty miles a day. Oxen could pull a wagon about ten to twelve miles in a ten hour day. That time is also tempered by one's health, the animal's health, the topography, the weather, and the availability to get food along the way. Oh, and, by the way, travel armed and avoid being outright killed or robbed on the way. Travel was dangerous in these days. There was little organized law, and a man defended himself and his family.

Atlanta to Washington, D.C. is roughly 624 miles, give or take. Today, Google estimates that time to be eleven hours by automobile. In 1779, that trip could take you about twenty days by foot, roughly eighteen days by horse, and forty one days by wagon…provided you or your horse did not get sick, and you didn't get dead somewhere along the way in those dark woods.

Another reason for staying home was more basic: most of us were farmers in the late 1700s. We could not venture away from our livestock unless we had a way for someone to cover for us. We worked from dawn 'til dusk in those days and pretty much huddled inside when it got dark. Candle and lanterns were our only sources of light, and they were expensive to buy and time-consuming to make. We did not burn fifteen candles in a room like you see in movies. If you were wealthy, you could splurge, but the common man could not afford the time and money it would take to use all of those candles.

(Point of trivia: In the late 1700s, candles were made from tallow, which a family obtained during the fall when they slaughtered their cows and sheep. This tallow was rendered from the fat; it was nasty, smoked, and smelled bad. Even as candles were improved and paraffin was developed in the mid-1800s, making candles was a job. A "Chandler" was a professional candle-maker in those days, and they were few in number, so one made their own as they could. You think your Dad had a fit when you didn't turn out the lights, try burning two candles when one was enough in a cabin back in 1840.)

In the novel *A Christmas Carol*, Ebenezer Scrooge guarded those lumps of coal like they were made of gold. They may as well have been. Coal, chopped firewood... all expensive, and labor intensive. Fuel was expensive in those times just as it is now.

Consider, too, we never traveled enough to get to know people outside of our sphere. What you saw off of your front porch was home... it was your world. Again, we lived and died within miles from our places of birth. Our worldly encounters were peddlers.

Because of the limited contact, people from the North and South became more regionalized over time; rumors, stories and just plain ignorant beliefs prevailed. There was a time when people up North thought that people in the South ran around half-naked and ate raw animals. People in the South believed that "Yankees got tails." I am not making this up. In written testimony after the George Wirz trial, witnesses insisted that they tried to see the tails on the Yankee prisoners being held at Camp Sumter (Andersonville). It became that extreme a notion. Fact is, people in the Deep South still believe that to some degree. (My uncle, in Alabama, swears he saw it first hand while he was in the army.)

With all of this ignorance, fear sets in. It is a strange, but true, characteristic about people. What people are ignorant of, they grow to fear. Fear is uncomfortable, so the mind steels itself with hate. Hate is a control for people. I do not have a degree in human psychology, either, but I have some insight; it seems rather logical to see this transition.

All throughout history, wars have been mongered by clever folks that used their population's ignorance about something. Adolph Hitler was a master at it. Tell people something that they know to be true, then, you can embellish and manipulate the masses with half-truths; works every time. That is how and why historical novels work. An author builds a fictional story around a commonly-known historical event, then, the whole story rings true.

We need to now understand what the early problems were, and how our ancestors began to splinter over issues that we are still having fits over. Those differences that were driven by distance and a lack of understanding became complicated and volatile.

We will take up the narrative with the next step toward the Civil War, The Articles of Confederation.

CHAPTER FOUR

THE ARTICLES OF CONFEDERATION

Originally, it was called "Articles of Confederation and Perpetual Union". This agreement was used by the original thirteen states to lock together in an organized way. It was a confederation of sovereign (independent) states, and served as its first constitution.

Definitions are the key in understanding just what we are trying to comprehend about this time. The term "sovereignty" is the focus here. A "sovereign state" is a political organization with a centralized government that has supreme, independent authority over all of its geographic area, period. These separate colonies were not agreeing to give authority to a central government except to that extent this compact stated. Every one of these states was still independent to themselves. These states had a permanent population, a government, and the capacity to enter into relations with other sovereign states. Nowhere in these agreements did any of these states turn over their total control to anyone else. It was a loose confederation... and it was a tenuous arrangement, at best.

Simply put, think of each of these former colonies as little nations. Today, it is almost impossible for people to read the word "state" without thinking in modern terms. We have to get past that mindset to understand what the South was talking about in the mid-nineteenth century. "State" meant "nation".

The Second Continental Congress convened on June 12, 1776, a day after appointing a committee to prepare a draft of the Declaration of Independence. This session of the Congress resolved to appoint a committee of 13 to prepare a draft of a constitution for a union of the states. The committee met repeatedly. The chairman, John Dickinson, presented their results to the Congress on July 12, 1776 (5 days after we signed the

66

Declaration). Debates grew hot and heavy and lasted long into the nights on such issues as sovereignty, the exact powers to be given the confederate government, and whether to have a judiciary, and voting procedures. There were those that wanted more control by a central government while others argued that that very issue was the reason the colonies were seeking a separation from England. The final draft of the Articles was prepared in the summer of 1777, and the Second Continental Congress approved them for ratification by the individual states on November 15, 1777.

In practice, the Articles were in use beginning in 1777; the final draft of the Articles served as the operating system of government used by the Congress ("the United States in Congress assembled") until it became the law by final ratification on March 1, 1781; at that point Congress became the "Congress of the Confederation".

Even when not yet ratified, the Articles provided domestic and international legitimacy for the Continental Congress to direct the American Revolutionary War, conduct diplomacy with Europe, and deal with territorial issues and Indian relations. Nevertheless, the weak government created by the Articles became a matter of concern for key nationalists. We need to now understand what the early problems were and how we handled them.

THE REAL FIRST PRESIDENT OF THE UNITED STATES

Here comes part of what they did not tell you....George Washington was not the first President of the United States. I know that's what everybody thinks, but keep in mind that we all used to think that if you swallowed a pumpkin seed, you'd grow one in your stomach.

John Hanson was the real first President of the United States. He was a merchant and public official from Maryland during the era of the American Revolution, and took a large role in the formation of our government and our affairs. It was in 1779, after serving in a variety of roles for the Patriot cause in Maryland, that John Hanson was elected as a delegate to the Continental Congress. He signed the Articles of Confederation in 1781 after Maryland finally joined the other states in ratifying them.

JOHN HANSON

In November of 1781, he was elected President of the Continental Congress, and became the first president to serve a one-year term under the provisions of the Articles of Confederation. It was Hanson who authorized The Great Seal of the United States. While George Washington is universally recognized by historians as the first President of the United States formed under the United States Constitution, it was Hanson who served as the first president with seven more to follow. Each served for one year under the Articles. It was after we ratified the Constitution that we elected George Washington... the ninth president of the United States. Here are the other presidents before George Washington:

John Hanson (November 5, 1781 thru November 3, 1782)

Elias Boudinot (November 4, 1782 thru November 2, 1783)

Thomas Mifflin (November 3, 1783 thru November 29, 1784)

Richard Henry Lee (November 30, 1784 thru November 22, 1785)

John Hancock (November 23, 1785 thru June 5, 1786)

Nathaniel Gorham (June 6, 1786 thru February 1, 1787)

Arthur St. Clair (February 2, 1787 thru January 21, 1788)

Cyrus Griffin (January 22, 1788 thru April 30, 1789)

Under the Articles, the states retained sovereignty over all governmental functions that were not specifically relinquished to the national government. Let us repeat that part...

THE STATES RETAINED <u>SOVEREIGNTY</u> OVER <u>ALL</u> GOVERNMENTAL FUNCTIONS NOT <u>SPECIFICALLY</u> RELINQUISHED TO THE NATIONAL GOVERNMENT.

What that means is simple enough; if it wasn't spelled out in the Articles, the boys in Congress had no authority to do it. This is not rocket science, it's pretty straight forward.

The individual Articles set the rules for current and <u>FUTURE</u> operations of the United States Government. This is one of the points that Jefferson Davis will hammer home later on. Our government was made capable of making war and peace, negotiating diplomatic and commercial agreements with foreign countries, and deciding disputes between the states, including their additional and contested western territories. That was it at that time.

Article XIII stipulated that "their provisions shall be inviolably observed by every state" and "the Union shall be perpetual". This little piece does not allow one without the other. If the "provisions" were not kept, the contract for a "perpetual union" would be null and void. This is a strong argument made by Davis later on. It is only common sense to conclude that one cannot pick and choose parts of a contract at their own whim. You cannot, they say, "have your cake and eat it, too".

When the 13 colonies rebelled against Great Britain in the War for American Independence, it was an act of secession, plain and simple. It is a little odd to think that we celebrate one act of secession, on "The Fourth of July", and vilify other Americans for the same act decades later. Hypocritical, isn't it?

During the Revolutionary War, each of the rebelling colonies regarded itself as a sovereign nation, as I have explained. They were cooperating with a dozen other sovereigns in a relationship of convenience to achieve shared goals, the most immediate being independence from Britain.

The Continental Congress passed the Articles of Confederation—"Certain Articles of Confederation and Perpetual Union"—to create "The United States of America". That document asserted that "Each State retains is sovereignty, freedom and independence" while entering into "a firm league of friendship with each other" for their common defense and to secure their liberties, as well as to provide for "their mutual and general welfare". No one gave up any local sovereignty.

Under the Articles of Confederation, the central government was weak, without even an executive to lead it. Its only political body was the Congress, which could not collect taxes or tariffs (it could ask states for "donations" for the common good). It did have the power to oversee foreign relations but could not create an army or navy to enforce foreign treaties. Even this relatively weak governing document was not ratified by all the states until 1781. It is an old truism that "All politics are local." and never was that more true than during the early days of the United States.

Having just seceded from what they saw as a despotic, powerful central government that was too distant from its citizens, Americans were skeptical about giving much power to any government other than that of their own States, where they could exercise more direct control. However, seeds of nationalism were also sown in the Revolutionary War. That war required a united effort, and many men who likely would have lived out their lives without venturing from their own state traveled to other states as part of the Continental Army. The remnants of that time will dangle like a ghostly shadow later in time, and will become the image that people will have of a Union, undivided.

The weaknesses of the Articles of Confederation were obvious almost from the beginning. Foreign nations, ruled to varying degrees by monarchies, were inherently contemptuous of the American experiment of entrusting rule to the ordinary people. A government without an army or navy and little real power was, to them, simply a laughing stock and a plum ripe for picking whenever the opportunity arose.

Domestically, the lack of any uniform codes meant each state established its own form of government, a chaotic system marked, at times, by mob rule that burned courthouses and terrorized state and local officials. State laws were passed and almost immediately repealed; sometimes ex post facto laws made new codes retroactive. Collecting debts could be virtually impossible.

George Washington, writing to John Jay in 1786, said, "We have probably had too good an opinion of human nature in forming our confederation". He underlined his words for emphasis. Jay himself felt the country had to become "one nation in every respect". Alexander Hamilton felt "the prospect of a number of petty states, with appearance only of union", was something "diminutive and contemptible".

In May 1787, a Constitutional Convention met in Philadelphia to address the shortcomings of the Articles of Confederation. Some Americans felt it was an aristocratic plot, but every state felt a need to do something to improve the situation, and smaller states felt a stronger central government could protect them against domination by the larger states. What emerged was a new Constitution: "in order to provide a more perfect union". It established the three branches of the federal government—Executive, Legislative, and Judicial—and provided for two houses within the Legislature. That Constitution, though amended 27 times, has governed the United States of America ever since. It failed to clearly address two critical issues, however.

It made no mention of the future of slavery. (The Northwest Ordinance, not the Constitution, prohibited slavery in the Northwest Territories, that area north of the Ohio River and along the upper Mississippi River.) It also did not include any provision for a procedure by which a state could withdraw from the Union, or by which the Union could be wholly dissolved. To have included such provisions would have been, as some have pointed out, to have written a suicide clause into the Constitution. But the issues of slavery and secession would take on towering importance in the decades to come, with no clear-cut guidance from the Founding Fathers for resolving them.

Following ratification by 11 of the 13 states, the government began operation under the new U.S. Constitution in March 1789. In less than 15 years, several New England states had already threatened to secede from the Union; yep, that is what I said, it was <u>New England that started the secession parade.</u>

New England has a no-nonsense attitude that Southerners have always had difficulty with. While Southerners are nice to folks to their face, they can have a catty streak that slices up people in a sweet way. The types of people that populated the North were, as we have explored, not the same as those in the South. I have always noticed that people settle where they tend to fit in best; one kind attracts another. The South attracts one type of personality, the North, another. That still applies today.

(This little bit of truth seems to be undetectable by our friends in Hollywood, as they seek to create their ideal America in their movies. I might add that some people in California wear too much spandex, eat tofu, and inject fat into their lips; point made.)

72

THE CONSTITUTIONAL CONVENTION OF 1787

The Constitution was adopted on September 17, 1787, by the Constitutional Convention in Philadelphia, Pennsylvania. It was ratified by conventions in eleven states and went into effect on March 4, 1789.

Delegates to the Constitutional Convention committed, above all else, to the creation of a viable union. They worked long hours to come to an agreement about the divisive subject of slavery in this new country. In the first of many compromises, delegates gained Southern support for the Constitution by recognizing and protecting slavery.

They did this in two ways:

1) The Three-Fifths Clause: *Article I, Section 2, Clause 3:* "Representatives and direct Taxes shall be apportioned among the several States which may be included within this Union, according to their respective Numbers, which shall be determined by adding to the whole Number of free Persons, including those bound to Service for a Term of Years, and excluding Indians not taxed, three fifths of all other Persons".

2) In the Constitutional provision for the return of runaway slaves. Although the issue of Slavery was addressed in this document, our founding fathers began the old trick of saying a lot and not saying anything.

The language dealing with this issue was so vague that it squeaked by ratification, and set us up for a war later on. Some things don't change, I guess; "you have to vote for it to see what's in it...?"

Simply put, Negroes would only be counted as three fifths of a human-being. The North argued, among other things, that if the South could count property, (slaves), then why couldn't the

Northern States count their property, (cows and pigs), for the same numerical calculations?

This attitude about equating Negroes and cows illustrates a point. Americans, both in the North and the South, had little respect for anyone who did not look like them; that was a fact. If contemporary writers don't own up to this, and continue to mask the brutal reality of it all, then they should get out of the history genre and get a job writing for a gardening publication.

This form of censorship has now worked its way into a lot of national historical sights. Living-historians and government employees at National Parks are told not to use the term "slave". They are instructed to use the term "servant", so as not to offend minorities; skew the language, distort the truth.

There is a lot of difference between a servant and a slave. If you mess with the words, you mess with history. Minority groups should embrace all of their history honestly. By editing the historical presentations, young people get a distorted view and are deprived of their own heritage. We are in the process of writing minorities out of history, again, with this insane process. It is literally "déjà vu" all over again. History does repeat itself.

(Point of trivia: Please be vigilant when you go to a National Battlefield. Those folks who work there are Government Employees and are being censored by a seriously "politically correct" establishment that is catering to the special interest groups we have talked about. The information they present is only part of the truth. I have caught a number of them at this little bit of re-write: at the Craven's House on the side of Lookout Mountain, we were told by a Park Official that the door leading into the dining room was short because Mr. Craven wanted his slaves to bow down to him as they came in. The missing piece of information that the people in our group were not told was that the house was rebuilt after the War in 1867. There were no slaves around when he built that door. This young African-American woman was caught up in her own personal agenda, and was

74

editorializing instead of sticking to the facts. I could write another book on this subject, alone....and, I probably will.)

THE ASSUMPTION ACT OF 1790

Congress passed the "Residence Act" as part of a compromise brokered between James Madison, Thomas Jefferson and Alexander Hamilton. Madison and Jefferson favored a southerly site for the capital on the Potomac River, but they lacked a majority to pass the measure through Congress. Hamilton was pushing for Congress to pass the Assumption Bill, to allow the Federal government to assume debts accumulated by the states during the American Revolutionary War. With the compromise, Hamilton made the deal work and allowed the passage of The Residence Act which gave authority to President George Washington to select an exact site for the capital.

Related threats of secession were already being bantered about by New England, and the pressure was on.

There were threats of a break-up of this new union if the Assumption Bill, which provided for the federal government to assume the debts of the various states, was not passed. The next Northern threat secession was over the expense of the Louisiana Purchase. Then, in 1812, President James Madison, the man who had done more than any other individual to shape the Constitution, led the United States into a new war with Great Britain.

The New England States objected, because war would cut into their trade with Britain and Europe. Resentment grew so strong that a convention was called at Hartford, Connecticut, in 1814, to discuss secession for the New England states. "The Hartford Convention" was the most serious secession threat up to that time, but its delegates took no action. New England set the template for secession; the South would use this opening and run with it.

THE MISSOURI COMPROMISE

The westward expansion of the United States caused more division. Abolitionists wanted no more slave states added, while pro-slavery advocates pushed for more. When Missouri applied for Statehood as a slave state in 1820, a compromise was struck.

A line was drawn from the southwestern corner of Missouri that extended across the continent on the 36th parallel, ending at California (Mexico). This line allowed future states above the line to come in as "free states", while states below the line would come in as "slave states". At the same time, Maine was brought in as a free state, bringing the count to 11 free states and 11 slave states. The balance was kept, and neither side lost any ground. This was known as the Missouri Compromise; very important.

Southerners had discussed secession in the nation's early years as had the folks up north; their concerns were not just about slavery. When push came to shove in 1832, it was not slavery, but tariffs that drove the agenda. A new tariff pushed by the North was going to edge us closer to a war.

National tariffs were proposed that would protect Northern manufacturers; this increased prices for European-manufactured goods purchased in the predominantly agricultural South. These were the dubbed the "Tariff of Abominations" in the South.

The man that led this anti-tariff movement was South Carolina's own, John C. Calhoun.

JOHN C. CALHOUN

CHAPTER FIVE

THE TARIFF OF 1828

This was a protective tariff passed by the Congress of the United States on May 19, 1828. It was designed to protect Northern industries. It was rebuked and opposed by the South, and was called "The Tarff of Abomination" because of the negative effects it had on the antebellum Southern economy.

These tariffs functioned as a protective blanket that was passed with the aid of Northern politicians to help protect a lot of Northern industries. These Northern manufacturers were being hit hard by cheaper European goods. They could not, or would not, compete with these foreign prices. These tariffs were an added tax on top of the imported items, making them equivalent to Northern prices in the market. This Tariff marked the high point of US tariffs.

This forced Southerners to pay higher prices on things they could not produce. It most cases, items cost the Southerners half again what they had been paying. Remember that the South had little manufacturing and depended on these imports for their daily lives. The second part of this dilemma was the effect this reduction of trade had on the British. The less the British could sell here, the less they were going to need Southern raw goods... cotton, rice, sugar cane, tobacco, and indigo. It was, in effect, a "double whammy". The South had grown accustomed to shipping its cotton to England and France in return for shiploads of manufactured items, including clothes made from their own cotton. Trade was brisk, and the profits high for the South on several levels.

Complicating all of this was the gradual build-up by the North. They were harnessing the abundant water power in New England to grow their own manufacturing base. It was not long before the North began turning out leather goods, iron, and steel products, as well as arms and munitions. Soon, the North also began to develop its own textile industries, along with pottery and furniture production. Fancy items in silver and gold were pouring out of New England, not to mention a thriving clock industry. The South was being forced to buy these Northern goods because the tariffs were making European goods too expensive. These prices, they felt, were exorbitant, and they resented being held up by greedy Northern manufacturers. As you can see, one thing leads to another...and that "another" was "The Nullification Act" introduced by South Carolina in late 1832. This would lead to the Nullification Crisis that began in late 1832.

Looking back with 20-20 vision, we can see that the South should have been building its own manufacturing base. Truth is, too many people got stuck in their ways, which was growing cotton, and did not see this coming. In 1830, an unidentified visitor to the South observed the relentless cycle of the planters' misuse of spare capital. They simply sold more cotton to buy more Negroes to sell more cotton to buy more Negroes to sell more cotton....and on and on it went. I have always the loved British sarcasm, and he nailed it.

This conflict in 1832 nearly touched off the war. South Carolina's great orator and Senator, John C. Calhoun, who was then running for Vice President, declared that States (his own State in particular) were under "no obligation to obey the Federal Tariff Law", or to collect it from ships entering its harbors. This was a big "in your face" to the authority in Washington.

President Andrew Jackson, (the gentleman on your twenty dollar bill), responded with a Proclamation of Force, declaring, "I consider, then, the power to annul a law of the United States, assumed by one state (sic), incompatible with the existence of the Union, contradicted expressly by the letter of the Constitution, inconsistent with every principle on which it was founded, and destructive of the great object for which it was formed."

Congress authorized Jackson to use military force, if necessary, to enforce the law. Every one of the Southern Senators walked out in protest before the vote was taken. Andrew Jackson ordered warships to the Charleston harbor; Charleston, and its leaders backed down, but not without a bad taste in their mouth for Yankee ships in their harbor. They were going to remember this for a long time to come....a long time.

South Carolina rescinded its Nullification Ordinance. This, though, was the first time a Southern State had threatened to secede.

STATES' RIGHTS

This incident set the stage for the "States' Rights" dispute, pitting State laws against the notion of Federal sovereignty. According to past agreements made with the founding fathers, Southerners held tight to their right to have Washington stay out of their affairs, unless this authority was backed by specific Constitutional Law. The South was not going to have a heavy hand from Washington impose what they perceived as an issue for the State. They would tolerate no Yankee interference on their Southern lifestyle.

Political parties began to spring up thru the South demanding stronger States' Rights. One family in Union, S.C., the Gists, got so hung up on the issue, that they named one of their sons "States Rights"; he was later killed near Franklin, Tennessee fighting for those very beliefs.

This issue over these tariffs caused an on-going feud between the North and South. Time did not heal all of the wounds, and insults to injuries did not fade away. It became genetic memory.

(I have to interject a story that my Great Grandmother told me when I was about four. She told me how the Yankees had come to her farm when she was a child and had stolen their chickens. That incident took place in 1865... this was a story told to me in 1954. I am telling you, Southerners do not forget. By the mid-1800s, Southerners began to think of themselves as not only different from Northerners, but living in their own country.)

NATIONAL LEADERSHIP

The folks up north had seen eight of the first eleven presidents come from this moneyed South. (We are counting the presidents under the new Constitution at this point.) In the North, there was a low, festering resentment that eight of the first eleven U.S. presidents were Southerners. They perceived, and rightly so, that the equation is this balance of power and regional interest was being dominated by Southerners; it was, indeed.

The South, at the same time, saw a serious problem with the way the North was pushing for more internal improvements and expansions paid for by all of the states with these various tariffs; in particular, roads, harbors, canals, etc. The South saw that they were on the short-side of the equation because most of these improvements were up North. They felt that all of the add-ons that benefited only Northern states were what we call "pork". Why should a planter in South Carolina pay for the construction of a Northern harbor... where was his up-side? "Pork is Pork", it doesn't matter if it smells like ham or clam chowder. New England was manipulating the monies in a very concentrated area.

THE ABOLITIONISTS

One has to remember that slavery was not a new issue across the board. Even before the Southern States were threatening to secede over the tariff issue, there was a growing and confusing chasm developing over the institution of Slavery.

Again, all of the original 13 colonies had been involved, to one degree or another, in slavery. This fact kept being thrown up in the face of Northern legislators who balked at this Southern interest. The three largest ports in our early history were Charleston, Boston, and New York City. The slave-trade flourished in all of these ports, just as other commerce had.

Early abolitionists, such as Benjamin Franklin and John Adams, had spoken out loudly about the evils of slavery. There had been heated arguments in the Continental Congress over this issue. Our founding fathers developed a trick that still goes on in Congress today; they stalled any action on it. They kept "kicking that can down the road". They were brave on the battlefield, but when they became Congressmen, many lost their spine.

The definition of our Congress soon became an on-going joke; when you looked up "The U.S. Congress" in the dictionary, it reads, "See spineless".

The Abolitionists were a small, but loud, minority that grew stronger over time. By the 1820s, they had turned into a full-fledged movement. They would not be silenced, and their message was heard loud-and-clear in Northern Churches. They printed and distributed thousands of pamphlets and newspapers. Their protestations created anti-slavery factions in Congress and elsewhere. It was all a matter of whose dog was in the fight.

At first, the abolitionists concluded that the best solution was to send the slaves back to Africa; they did not advocate for the Africans to stay in the United States. A group called "The American Colonization Society" raised monies and established a haven for those blacks who wanted to return to Africa in 1820. This small nation, Liberia, still exists today and English is still its official language.

(Point of trivia: 88 countries have English as their national language; the United States is not one of those. German was once proposed as our national language; the feeling, in 1780, was that any national language would be "undemocratic", and serious debates about a national language were dismissed.)

81

Over time, the issue of slavery became more engulfing and more retrospect than just "evil". By the early 1840s, it became a "moral wrong" for some. The abolitionists began to agitate and push their cause by using that "evil" as their motivation.

You can imagine how this bothered and outright heated up Southern Christians in the Deep South. They did not like reading about how scandalous and wicked they were. Who were these strangers, and what gave them the right to judge them? This provoked, among other things, religious break-ups. In the mid-1840s, the American Methodist and Baptist Churches split into Northern and Southern denominations. (Somehow, the Presbyterians hung together, but it was a strain.) All the while, the Episcopal Church remained a Southern stronghold and a "firebrand" bastion among the wealthy and planter classes. Robert E. Lee and Jefferson Davis will be counted among this group.

The Catholics also maintained their solidarity. (A lot of 19th century Americans had a dim view of Catholics at this time, and proposed that their loyalty was to their Pope, and not this country or their state.)

Abolitionist literature began showing up in the Southern mails. Southerners were offended by this intrusion into their personal lives and feared that these writings would somehow fuel a slave uprising. They had reasons to feel this way because of slave revolts that had happened earlier in Haiti, Jamaica, and Louisiana.

Earlier, more than 200 slaves, led by a slave named Charles Deslondes and two other influential slaves, rose up, and, brandishing hoes, axes and clubs, they began a march towards New Orleans. They burned 5 plantations, (three completely), and several store houses and sugar houses. They were stopped near present day Kenner, Louisiana by the militia. Many were executed; fear still continued to lurk in the minds of Southerners.

NAT TURNER

More recently, and a lot closer to home for a lot of Virginians, was the 1831 incident with a slave named Nat Turner. He had led other slaves in Southeast Virginia on a rampage and ended up killing 55 to 65 people, mostly women and small children. Reports stated that the victims were "hacked to pieces". Southerners knew there was trouble coming. As far as they were concerned, any Southern blood spilled by any slave was a direct attack by the North. They blamed it all on Yankees.

THE MEXICAN WAR

Other elements began to change the political landscape of the time. The Mexican War added huge territories to the western part of the United States, creating even more complications to the spread of Slavery. It was an example of how "Manifest Destiny" was getting a boost from the American bayonet. The abolitionists called this a grab by the "slave power" advocates, and they wanted it stopped.

In response to this trend, A Pennsylvania Congressman, David Wilmot, submitted an Amendment to a Mexican War funding bill. Wilmot's Proposal divided both parties along sectional lines. This Pennsylvania Representative was adamantly against the extension of slavery to lands ceded by Mexico. His proposal to Congress on August 8, 1846 would further divide Congress by drawing another line on slavery. This proposal stated "neither slavery nor involuntary servitude shall ever exist" in lands won in the Mexican-American War.

This was going to go over like a lead balloon to those who believed in Slavery and its extension. This proposal never passed into law, but it told Southerners that the Northern Agitators were going to cut off their economy piece by piece. There would be no more meaningful compromises. The South began to see the writing on the wall; these abolitionists were not going to stop.

THE FUGITIVE SLAVE ACT OF 1850

On September 9, 1850, to the consternation of Southerners, California was admitted into the Union as a Free State. This happened because the pressure from Gold Rush miners who did not want to find themselves in competition with slave labor. This change in numbers threw the balance of power to the Northern States.

At this point in American history, national politics had become almost entirely sectional, a dangerous business, pitting North against South—and vice versa. This applied itself in practically all matters, however remote.

To soothe the Southern faction over the admission of California as a Free State, Congress passed the Fugitive Slave Act in 1850. This act made all Northerners personally responsible for the returns of runaway slaves. This knee-jerk, ill-conceived move was made by a misguided Congress in a panic to placate the South.

Some things just never change. This law made it illegal to "house" any slave, "aid" any slave, or "see" a slave and not report it. Like I said earlier, whenever Congress gets an idea, things are bound to get worse. This was a classic move in a series of moves that Congress will pass to push us faster into a National Catastrophe. It's the time-proven line, "I'm from the Government, and I'm here to help".

ANTHONY BURNS

Anthony Burns was a runaway slave who had settled in Boston. He had educated himself, sought and found employment, and was living a good life working in a clothing store. Someone turned him in to the newly formed police force that this new law had created. Burns was dragged publicly from the clothing store and thrown into jail. Word spread, emotions began to boil, and abolitionists, as well as others, tried to get him freed. He and his case became the new rallying point for Northern Abolitionists. This was just what the abolitionists were looking for. This was a law that would not be tolerated by an already over-stressed group of activists, and this was going to recruit even more help.

Burns was not released. He was eventually placed back into shackles and hauled south to Virginia, returned to his rightful owners. Needless to say, this whole affair re-kindled the fire against slavery, and did bring a whole new group of people into the argument. Folks who had not paid any attention before began to get interested in the plight of people like Anthony Burns. This incident put a "face" on those enslaved.

Burns was eventually purchased and set free by a group of abolitionists shortly after he was returned to Virginia; this affair kept the pressure up on the slavers. Anthony Burns was now a part of the daily discourse on slavery and its evils.

Southerners read about the issue in a different perspective. Burns was "property", and the law was the law. He should have been returned to his rightful owners. Again, in their minds, Northern agitators were poking their abolitionist noses in areas that they had no legal right to. They reasoned that we either have laws or we don't. Northerners were adhering to the laws they wanted, and were ignoring the rest. This was not settling well down South. How arrogant could the North be?

In their minds, Southerners believed that anarchy gets a foot in the door in this manner. This country, they debated, was founded on laws, and that those laws could be changed by a set system of procedures. There was a process to redress a need to alter or delete a law. They felt that activists of any kind subvert the process by not adhering to the law. This radical approach creates a dangerous climate. In the Southern mind of the mid-19th Century, these abolitionists were flirting with treason.

On the other side of the coin, can you imagine how this new law was a slap in the face of all of the abolitionists? Now it made Northerners, who didn't want to put a dog in the fight, to do just that. Northerners were forced to either break the law or become slavery advocates. Congress, in effect, actually began to divide the North against itself, as well.

A TENNESSEE CRACK

In 1850, down South, the Nashville Convention met from June 3 through June 12 "to devise and adopt some mode of resistance to northern aggression". While the delegates approved 28 resolutions affirming the South's Constitutional Rights within the new western territories and similar issues, they essentially adopted a wait-and-see attitude before taking any drastic action.

Compromise measures at the Federal level diminished interest in a second Nashville Convention, but a much smaller meeting was held in November. It approved measures that affirmed the right of secession but rejected any unified secession among Southern states.

During his brief Presidency, pro-secession advocates approached President Taylor about their interests. Taylor flew into a rage and declared he would raise an army, put himself at its head, and force any state that attempted secession back into the Union. Some Southerners were not yet convinced that a split in the Union was the right move.

THE GREAT POTATO FAMINE

Most folks have forgotten the role that a great European agricultural calamity played in the course of our country's fate. The potato famine that struck Ireland and Germany in the 1840s–1850s sent waves of starving and desperate immigrants to America's shores. This will change the economic dynamics; more of them settled in the North than in the South.

The South was way too hot, it was loaded with mosquitoes, and the work just didn't pay well enough for one to put up with all of the miserable conditions. Slave labor in the South kept labor wages low, and the Irish and German immigrants could not, and would not compete with that kind of competition.

I believe that if air-conditioning had not been invented, the current population in Atlanta would be about twelve people. Southern weather was always a factor in the low immigration numbers. After air-conditioning became so widely used, Southern numbers began to increase. All of a sudden, folks from up North decided that snow and ice could be avoided in the suburbs of Southern cities.

These European newcomers in the 1840s and 1850s had sought refuge in the "United States", not in "New York" or "Virginia" or "Louisiana". To most of them, the U.S. was a single entity, not a collection of sovereign nations. Arguments in favor of secession failed to move them, for the most part. They were desperate for work and food, and politics didn't put a potato in the pot.

These new immigrants are the folks who became the new "Negroes" of the North. They slowly, but surely, began to replace all of the remaining roles of slaves in the North. It was a fact that an Irishman would work for pennies and did not have to be kept. His labor was almost free to those factory owners in the Northern cities. If you have not seen the movie "*Gangs of New York*", you need to get it. It is based on a real story of the Irish immigrants that landed between 1845 and 1864. It really does show you how poorly treated these immigrants were...great costumes, and a really close look at that time period. This is a rare effort out of Hollywood. I recommend this one.

Slavery simply played out in an employment-rich North, and to put it in historical perspective, the people in the North had no more interest in the plight of Blacks than did the South. They wanted nothing more to do with them than any Whites in 19th Century America; Blacks simply were not equal in any respect.

As a matter of fact, Whites in the North and the South generally classified most foreigners in the same way: There was Irish-trash, Black-trash, and Chinese-trash...they were all "trash". That is the way it was. We, as a nation, were a long way from any kind of equality. We were slowly engaging with each other in areas where it could not be avoided, but we were a long way from Selma, Alabama.

UNCLE TOM'S CABIN

HARRIET BEECHER STOWE

During the 1850s, one event after another, even the day-to-day matters, seemed to galvanize and push people further apart. Things turned worse in 1852 when a woman by the name of Harriett Beecher Stowe published a book called *Uncle Tom's Cabin*.

Mrs. Stowe was raised by a hardcore Congregationalist father and mother. She came by her abolitionists leanings honestly and early in life. She was born in Connecticut and was influenced early in life by her brother, Henry Ward Beecher, who was a famous preacher and a leader in the Abolitionist Movement.

In 1832, Harriet Beecher Stowe lived with her family in Cincinnati, a border city in the free state of Ohio across the river from the slave state of Kentucky; here she was exposed to all the dichotomies of freedom and slavery. The passage, in 1850, of the Fugitive Slave Law led to turmoil in Ohio as free blacks and fugitives alike were seized. Stowe's family and many of their friends had long been abolitionists, and were inflamed by the injustice of the Fugitive Slave Law. Harriet began to write what were intended as a few sketches for an abolitionist newspaper. Begun as a serial in the *National Era*, she was destined, I think, to write what she did.

Uncle Tom's Cabin depicted slavery in the South as a horrible, sinful and downright evil institution. Needless to say, it influenced a lot of Northerners who had never taken the time to learn about slavery, or care about what went on in the South. Remember, the North and South had become almost two distinct countries, and communication and interrelationships between the North and South were rare. The book sold hundreds of thousands of copies, and opened up a Pandora's Box of emotions.

Northern passions were inflamed while furious Southerners, who were fit to be tied. They dismissed the story completely as an outrageously skewed and utterly unfair portrayal. (After the conflict began, it was said that Lincoln, upon meeting Mrs. Stowe, remarked, "So you are the little lady who started this Great

War?") New battle lines were drawn over this book, and tempers were even shorter. Everyone had an opinion about this missive.

THE KANSAS-NEBRASKA ACT

Illinois Senator Stephen A. Douglas sponsored a bill in 1854 that would overturn the Missouri Compromise, and permitted settlers in the Kansas Territory to choose for themselves whether they wanted a Free or Slave State. Outraged Northern abolitionists, horrified at the notion of slavery spreading by popular sovereignty, began raising funds to send anti-slave settlers to Kansas.

Outraged Southerners sent their own settlers, and a hardcore group known as "Border Ruffians", from slave-holding Missouri, went into Kansas to make trouble for the abolitionists. Into this volatile mix came an abolitionist-fanatic named John Brown riding with his sons and a gang. As the murders and massacres began to pile up, newspapers throughout the land carried headlines of "Bleeding Kansas." (The press has always loved to promote the bloody side of life.)

In the halls of Congress, the slavery issue had prompted feuds, insults, duels and finally a divisive gag rule that forbade even discussion or debate on petitions about the issue of slavery. During the Kansas controversy, a confrontation between a Senator and a Congressman stood out as really astounding and illustrated where we, as nation, were headed.

CHARLES SUMNER   **PRESTON BROOKS**

In 1856, Charles Sumner, a 45-year-old Massachusetts Senator and abolitionist, conducted a three-hour rant in the Senate chamber against the Kansas-Nebraska Act. He made it personal by focusing, in particular, on 59-year-old South Carolina Senator Andrew Butler. Sumner, a man of little tact and few manners in the eyes of the Southern Senators, mocked and compared the Southerner Butler to a pimp, "having taken as his mistress the harlot, Slavery".

The first thing the North has to understand, I might interject here, is that Southerners, then or now, do not take kindly to anyone messing with their kin or their reputation, no matter if it's true or not. Blood will follow, I guarantee it. We may have horse thieves in the family, but we take care of our own.

Two days later, Congressman Preston Brooks, a nephew of the demeaned South Carolinian, had heard what had happened and decided that some 'ole boy needed a good old-fashioned whipping. Brooks appeared beside Sumner's desk in the Senate and then caned him nearly to death with a gold-headed gutta-percha walking stick. The Northern Senator never did give Butler any more trouble.

By 1856, every respectable-sized town, North and South, had a half-dozen newspapers each; even small towns had at least one or more. The amazing and revolutionary new telegraph brought the latest news overnight or sooner. Throughout the North, the caning incident triggered profound indignation that was transformed into support for a new anti-slavery political party. Meanwhile, down South, South Carolinians began to mail Mr. Brooks more canes. You have to love the Southern passion.

THE REPUBLICAN PARTY IS BORN

JOHN C. FREMONT

The Republican Party grew out of the conflicts regarding the expansion of slavery into the new Western territories. The Kansas-Nebraska Act served as the unifying agent for abolitionists and split both the Democrats and the Whig Party. "Anti-Nebraska" protest meetings spread rapidly throughout the country.

Two such meetings were held in Ripon, Wisconsin, on February 28 and March 20, 1854. They were attended by groups of abolitionists, Free Soilers (sic), Democrats, and Whigs. They decided to call themselves Republicans because they professed to be political descendants of Thomas Jefferson's Democratic - Republican Party. The name was formally adopted by a state convention held in Jackson, Michigan on July 6, 1854.

In the election of 1856, the new Republican Party ran explorer John C. Fremont, the famed "Pathfinder", for president. Even though he lost, the party, itself, became a force to be reckoned with; Fremont ran again in 1864 with no real effect on the election. His political days were over.

One of these new faces in the Republican Party was Abraham Lincoln. The rail-splitter from Illinois became the new kid in town.

THE DRED SCOTT DECISION

DRED SCOTT

The fate of a nation was in the hands of a middle-aged man who had spent his entire life in servitude. Dred Scott was born sometime around the turn of the 19th century, often fixed at 1795, in Southampton County, Virginia. Legend has it that his name was Sam, but when his elder brother died, he adopted his name instead.

His parents were slaves, but it is uncertain whether the Blow family owned him at his birth or thereafter. Peter Blow and his family relocated first to Huntsville, Alabama, and then to St. Louis, Missouri. After Peter Blow's death, in the early 1830s, Scott was sold to a U.S. Army doctor named John Emerson.

In 1836, Scott fell in love with a slave of another army doctor. She was a 19 year-old beauty named Harriett Robinson. Her ownership was transferred over to Dr. Emerson when they were wed. Scott and his wife had two sons and two daughters.

In the ensuing years, Dr. Emerson traveled to Illinois and the Wisconsin Territories, both of which prohibited slavery. When Emerson died in 1846, Scott tried to buy freedom for himself and his family from Emerson's widow, but she refused.

Dred Scott made history by launching a legal battle to gain his freedom.

His contacts with St. Louis area abolitionists had given Scott hopes that he might be freed by using a past agreement called the "Missouri Compromise". The abolitionists convinced him that he was free because his owners had used him illegally above the 36th parallel line. The fact that he had lived with Dr. Emerson in free territories should, they told him, nullify his status as a slave.

The process began in 1846: Scott lost in his initial suit in a local St. Louis district court, but he won in a second trial, only to have that decision overturned by the Missouri State Supreme Court. With support from local abolitionists, Scott filed another suit in federal court in 1854, against John Sandford, the widow Emerson's brother and executor of his estate. When that case was decided in favor of Sandford, Dred Scott, with the aid of the abolitionists, turned to the U.S. Supreme Court.

In December 1856, Abraham Lincoln delivered a speech, foreshadowing the Emancipation Proclamation of 1863, examining the constitutional implications of the Dred Scott Case. The entire nation was watching this case; there was much at stake for both sides.

On March 6, 1857, the Supreme Court decision in *Dred Scott v. Sandford* was issued, 11 long years after the initial suits. Seven of the nine judges agreed with the outcome delivered by Chief Justice Roger Taney, who announced that slaves were not citizens of the United States and therefore had no rights to sue in Federal courts: "... They had no rights which the white man was bound to respect." Most of the judges held slaves and this was predictable.

The court ruled, in essence, that a slave was not a citizen, or even a person, and that slaves were "so far inferior that they [have] no rights which the white man [is] bound to respect." This was a reality in 1857. Blacks simply were not real humans to most Whites, admittedly or otherwise.

Southerners were relieved that they could now move their slaves in and out of free territories and states without losing them, while, in the North, the ruling merely drove more people into the anti-slavery camp. The big bang was about to happen. This was the spark that will lead us to war. Dred Scott had just started a war and did not even know it.

JOHN BROWN

In 1859, John Brown, of Bleeding Kansas notoriety, staged a murderous raid on the U.S. arsenal at Harpers Ferry, Virginia. He was hoping to inspire a general slave uprising that would purge the evil institution from this nation once and forever. The raid was thwarted by U.S. troops, commanded by Virginia's own Robert E. Lee. The slave revolt never happened.

John Brown was tried for treason and hanged. When it became public knowledge that he had been financed by Northern abolitionists, Southern anger was profuse and furious—especially after the Northern press elevated Brown to the status of hero and martyr. How dare these Northern tyrants exalt a common criminal that threatened their very homes and families? It simply reinforced the Southern conviction that Northerners were out to destroy their way of life. The South steadied itself for a long hard fight. They knew it was coming, and a lot of them welcomed it.

As the crucial election of 1860 approached, there arose more talk of Southern secession by a group of "fire-eaters"— influential orators who insisted Northern "fanatics" intended to free slaves "by law if possible, by force if necessary." Their rhetoric was inflammatory and full of dark omens of rape and slave uprisings. Southern homes would be looted and women and children placed in harm's way.

Bullying abolitionist newspapers and Northern orators (known as Black, or Radical Republicans) provided ample fodder for that conclusion. These Southern boys had about had it. Christians in the South could not be swayed by the moral argument by the North against slavery. Has anybody read 1 Timothy: 6: 1-2? I will quote it, later, with other verses that show that the Bible seemed to support slavery. Let us keep in mind that these people lived in a different time, and ours is not to judge, but to comprehend.

The 1850s drew to a close in near social convulsion and the established political parties began to break apart. This is always a dangerous sign. The Whigs simply vanished into other parties; the Democrats split into Northern and Southern contingents, each with its own slate of candidates. A Constitutional Union party also appeared, looking for votes from moderates in the Border States. As a practical matter, all of this assured a victory for the Republican candidate, Abraham Lincoln, who was widely, if wrongly, viewed in the South as a rabid abolitionist. With the addition of Minnesota (1858) and Oregon (1859) as Free States, the Southerners' greatest fears were about to be realized— complete control of the federal government by free-state, anti-slavery politicians.

With the vote split four ways, Lincoln and the Republicans swept into power in November 1860, gaining a majority of the Electoral College, but only a 40 percent plurality of the popular vote. It didn't matter to the South. In short order, always pugnacious South Carolina voted to secede from the Union, followed by six other Deep South states that were invested heavily in cotton. Game on. The South was leaving the Union, and Lincoln be damned! Yankees be damned! God save the South!

ABRAHAM LINCOLN

The Southern fear of Lincoln taking office and immediately ending slavery was unfounded, except in the minds of the riled-up slave owners. Lincoln's disgust of the institution of slavery did not consume him to the point of becoming irrational. There were a number of factors that he and the North had to deal with.

Lincoln was more determined to preserve the Union than he was committed to ending Slavery. His public remarks indicated that to those that would read them through unfiltered glasses. That being said, the South had no interest in trusting Lincoln; they had read other parts of his speeches, as well. Most Southerners did not believe Lincoln as he offered, time after time, that he would not interfere with the institution of Slavery. Lincoln had earlier attached himself to the anti-slavery Republican Party, and he did say over and over again in his election debates that a nation could not exist "half free and half slave". Remember his words:

"Either the opponents of slavery will arrest the further spread of it, and place it where the public mind shall rest in the belief that it is in course of ultimate extinction; or its advocates will push it forward, till it shall become alike lawful in all the States, old as well as new-- North as well as South".

Politicians seem to forget that some people have longer memories than they think. The South knew Lincoln's motives.

Some politicians suffer from a malady called S.M.S. (split-mouth syndrome). They can actually talk out of both sides of their mouths at the same time. (Native Americans called it a "Forked Tongue".) The question is always: "Which version of their truth are you to believe?"

First, and foremost, you have to fully understand that Lincoln, as President, could not single-handedly free the slaves. That was a Constitutional issue. Even his Emancipation Proclamation is up for debate. What power was he using when he made this proclamation? How legal was it? I have heard lawyers argue this for years, and I am not convinced that it was legal to interfere in the affairs of a foreign country, and The Confederate States of America was just as legitimate and the United States.

Jefferson Davis understood the Constitution, and his two books, *"The Rise and Fall of The Confederate Government"* and *" A Short History of The Confederate States of America"*, explain, in detail, how he and others would argue this point.

Every Southerner should have a copy of those two books at their bedside. You can get them on line anywhere. Read them carefully.

This legal debate is still going on today. Slavery was mentioned and protected several ways in the Constitution, and it was part of the fabric of our nation. Amendments are the means by which we, as citizens, can change laws. This issue was bigger than the office of the President. It needed the full vote of the people; Lincoln knew this, said this, yet modern educators look at him as if he was some "rock star" and believe only what they want to.

Lincoln could not see how the issue could be handled politically, but he also knew that there was an end-around option. If it was, indeed, impossible to get this institution killed outright by a political move, they could choke it off by limiting its spread into new territories. He wanted an end to this institution, and he was angling for ways around the greatest obstacle in his way, which was the Constitution.

Let me explain just how this would work. First, by stopping the addition of more potentially slave-voting states in Congress, they could weaken the power of the slave-holding faction, simply by adding more Free States and fewer Slave States. But, more importantly, the slave population was exploding.

From the late 1700s, when there were a few hundred thousand slaves in the country, the slave population had grown to three and a half million. If you look at the rate of increase in the population, Blacks would more than overwhelm whites in just a few years and their practical use as a labor force would become an impractical matter. Where were the whites going to use them, and how could they feed and clothe that many extra slaves? Slavery would eventually eat itself from within if more territories were not allowed to absorb the increased numbers.

The South could not survive economically without expansion. It was that simple; grow or die.

The Southern Press laid Lincoln out. He was vilified in the press, including outright lies and half-truths. They claimed that he would free the slaves and the end result would be anarchy, rapes, and looting. The journalists were right about Lincoln and his abolitionist views, but they kept missing his other focus on the Union. Some, in the Northern Press, were doing the same.

THE FREEDMEN'S BUREAU

(Point of trivia: Some of the South's fears did materialize after the War in the resulting "Re-Construction". The end result of the Emancipation did end up with a lot of looting and unpunished murders brought on by members of the Freedmen's Bureau and white partisans throughout the South. The Freedmen's Bureau was set up after the War to aid the re-settlement of the Negroes. This group was also a tool used by the North to further bring rebuke onto those that had formerly been their masters. This was not done as a public policy, rather as a collective of individual actions by members of the Republican Party and their radical element. Reconstruction was a nice finale for this war, and most of it will be swept under the Northern Rug.)

In any event, Southerners, in 1860, took it all in and were stirred into a frenzy by the unchecked Press. If there is a case to be made on what caused the Civil War, the Southern Press and its editors would be among the first to get the blame. This factor is probably the main reason so many non-slave holders were eager to join the ranks; they felt a personal threat by the Northern agitators.

Fewer than one out of three Confederate soldiers held slaves. According to the U.S. Census, in 1860, only 26% of the South held slaves; one also has to factor in the number of Blacks and Indians who held slaves. Their numbers are included in that number. It wasn't slavery that the soldiers were fighting for; it was the thought that a bunch of freed slaves and a foreign army would

100

have their way with the South. They had a real fear that this scenario would play out, and it did, later on... "Re-Construction".

One also has to consider that a lot of the wealthy slave owners had a fear that if things went badly in a war, they would be ruined. They considered the two futures, and neither looked bright. Southern Pride and Family Tradition played a major role in their thinking. Southerners will cut off their noses to spite their faces in some cases. I can attest to that, personally. We have a stubborn streak that runs deep in Dixie.

These planters, these "Southern Gentlemen", finally pitched in with both fists, one holding money, the other holding a rifle musket.

Let us not overlook the part the Northern Press had in this as well; maybe not to the extent of the Southern Press, but their editorials and promotion of the evils on the plantations added fuel to the fire. The Northern Press pictured Southerners as heartless, vicious, and uncivilized. Keep in mind that the 19th Century was a different time, and public image mattered.

After more than ten years of this badgering in the North and South, most folks had a firm idea about the other side, imagined or real: again, perception is reality. One elderly Tennessean later expressed it this way: "I wish there was a river of fire a mile wide between the North and the South, that would burn with unquenchable fury forevermore, and that it could never be passable to the endless ages of eternity by any living creature".

The immediate cause of Southern secession, therefore, was a fear that Lincoln and the Republican Congress would have abolished the institution of slavery. This would have ruined fortunes, wrecked the Southern economy, and left the South to contend with millions of freed blacks; that is exactly what happened.

Who, in their right mind, would vote for a man that would bankrupt them, their family, and destroy all that they were? This is not an elaboration; look at the final results to the South; absolute poverty, courtesy of the U.S. Government.

In 1860, Southerners had come to believe that there was no future in "US". The two regions were going to have to wing it alone, and negotiate trade and travel as any two other nations would do. They saw a European model forming in this region.

Lincoln believed that if the South was allowed to simply leave, that the nation would not survive. An immediate reason was the income that the Southern States created. We were not a manufacturing nation in 1860. We were an agricultural-exporting nation, and the South produced most of the income for the Federal Government through tariffs and duties. There was also a strong trade-driven commerce that fueled the income of a select group of Northern businessmen that was based on this money.

There simply was little chance the War could have been avoided. There were just too many years of mistrust, suspicions, and hatred that had built up... going back all the way to the formation of this country. Debts, real and imagined, were coming due. We were going to cash that check with more than 600,000 lives.

The Lincoln administration was able to squash a number of earlier secession movements in the Border States by the use of political tactics, force and literally violating the Constitution. We will explore just what those actions were later. Understand that Lincoln's current image has been filtered and sanitized by Northern books for a long time. We are about to open a few doors.

The South was going to war. Mr. Lincoln was not going to let the South leave. One Southern woman stated, "We have hated each other so. If we could only separate, a 'separation a *l'agreable,'* as the French say it, and not have a horrid fight for divorce".

Things had come a long way during the nearly 250 years since the Dutchman delivered his cargo of African slaves to the wharf at Jamestown. In 1860, almost everyone agreed that a war wouldn't last long and most thought it would be over by summertime. Some folks couldn't wait to have things put to right. GOD PRESERVE THE UNION! ....GOD SAVE THE SOUTH!

THE VAMPIRE.

Abe.—"COLUMBIA, THOU ART MINE, WITH THY BLOOD I WILL RENEW MY LEASE OF LIFE—AH! AH!"

CHAPTER SIX

THE ROAD TO 1860

LINCOLN   **BRECKINRIDGE**   **BELL**   **DOUGLAS**

1860 PRESIDENTIAL CANDIDATES

THE VOTE IN 1860

In April of 1860, the Democrats gathered in Charleston, South Carolina to select their candidate for president. The event was "ordered confusion" at best, and "controlled chaos" in the end. Northern Democrats felt that Stephen Douglas had the best chance to defeat the "BLACK REPUBLICANS." Pro–slavery candidate Douglas was considered a traitor to Southern Democrats because of his support for popular sovereignty, permitting states to choose for themselves their own choice of slave or no slaves. The Southern Democrats stormed out of the convention in the end, refusing to choose a delegate. Six weeks later, the Northern Democrats chose Douglas, while at a separate convention, the Southern Democrats, nominated then Vice President John C. Breckinridge.

The Republicans met in Chicago that May. Many were astute to conclude that Democrat's turmoil actually gave them a chance to take the election. They needed to select a candidate who could carry the North and win a majority of the Electoral College.

Republicans needed someone who could carry New Jersey, Illinois, Indiana and Pennsylvania. These four important states remained uncertain. There were a number of potential candidates, but, in the end, Abraham Lincoln of Illinois had emerged as the best choice. His debates with Douglas had made him a national figure and the publication of those debates in early 1860 made him even better known. He was nominated on the third ballot.

The elections in 1860 saw the new Republican Party win many seats in Congress. The Republicans were definitely not a National Party; rather they had their strength in the Northern States. They had very little support among Southerners. Abraham Lincoln won the presidency in 1860. Republicans opposed the expansion of slavery into the territories, and many party members were abolitionists who wanted to see the "peculiar institution" ended everywhere in the United States. This was what the Southern voter was keenly aware of, and it frightened them as well as angered them.

A number of aging politicians and distinguished citizens, calling themselves the CONSTITUTIONAL UNION PARTY nominated a wealthy slaveholder named, JOHN BELL, of Tennessee, as their candidate for President. This party stood for moderation and wanted to take no side in the issue.

With four candidates in the field, Lincoln received only 40% of the popular vote and 180 electoral votes — enough to narrowly win the crowded election. This meant that 60% of the voters selected someone other than Lincoln. This wasn't a mandate. After the results were tallied, the question was, 'Would the South accept the outcome'?

Most folks, who understood the South, saw the writing on the wall. If Lincoln was elected, he would allow the Republicans to phase out slavery and throw them all out in the streets... and who, again, in their right minds, would elect a man president that would send them into bankruptcy? That was what was at stake.

Money and politics are the same for most people. Vote for the money, always. Nothing has changed....nothing.

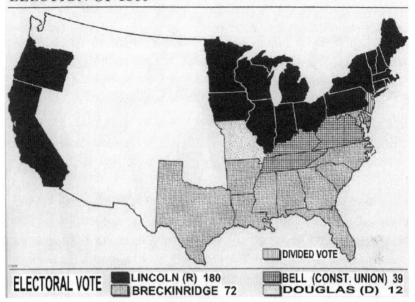

| ELECTORAL VOTE | LINCOLN (R) 180 | BELL (CONST. UNION) 39 |
| | BRECKINRIDGE 72 | DOUGLAS (D) 12 |

DIVIDED VOTE

SECESSION

South Carolina decided that it had had enough of this threat to its honor and its economy. They would not stand idly by and let these Northern States and Mr. Lincoln simply destroy them. South Carolina would secede.

There are three rules of life that still apply today:

1) Don't mess with a man's wife.

2) Don't mess with a man's dog.

3) Don't mess with a man's wallet.

South Carolina could do the math; they did not believe for a minute that The Republican Party would stop at just preventing the spread of slavery. They understood the age-old adage: let the nose of the camel into the tent; the rest would get in, eventually.

107

On November 22, 1860, a Convention of Secessionists gathered in a tiny town in western South Carolina. There, in a private residence, in Abbeville, a committee drew up and endorsed a petition for South Carolina to secede. The huge crowd that waited outside was beside itself over the idea that they were going to let Mr. Lincoln and his friends know that South Carolina was walking out of the Union.

Abbeville, itself, had a history of causing trouble that went way back to the people who settled there, the Huguenots.

The Huguenots were members of the Protestant Reformed Church of France during the 16th and 17th centuries. French Protestants were inspired by the writings of John Calvin in the 1530s, and they were called Huguenots by the 1560s. By the end of the 17th century, and into the 18th century, roughly 500,000 Huguenots had fled France during a series of religious persecutions. They relocated to Protestant nations, including the United States. It was in this area that a more familiar name was born, a man named John C. Calhoun. He came from good, trouble-making, free-thinking roots.

The Petition for Secession was taken to Columbia, South Carolina, the State's capitol. The First Baptist Church, on what is now Hampton Street, was the site of the first State Convention to discuss secession following the election of Abraham Lincoln as President of the United States. It was chosen because it was the largest meeting place in Columbia.

Under the chairmanship of D. F. Jamison, a unanimous vote of 159-0 in favor of secession on December 17, 1860 led to South Carolina seceding from the United States; it was the only such convention where the vote to secede was unanimous.

This convention lasted only one day, as Columbia was then experiencing an outbreak of smallpox. South Carolina's Order of Secession would not be signed until the delegates from this convention reconvened in Charleston, South Carolina, on December 20, 1860.

Columbia's little First Baptist Church was where the power brokers of South Carolina first declared that the state would secede. When the Northern Army invaded Columbia, they set fire to the Washington Street Methodist Church South. They had been led by the black First Baptist Church sexton who thought that it was the site of the secession convention. The invaders burned a third of Columbia's buildings, but the First Baptist Church was spared.

(Point of trivia: This Church is still there and welcomes visitors to see the original chapel, its furnishings and touch the table used in the drawing up of the document. I have touched it several times... it is the Real Southern Holy Grail.)

(Point of trivia: During the occupation of Columbia, an unidentified Union soldier threw a brick at the statue of George Washington that was located on the steps of the capitol; it broke off the lower section of Washington's cane. That statue is still there, unrepaired, with a plaque close by that explains the story and lets the visitor know that those Yankees can come back and fix it. The folks in South Carolina still have a long memory.)

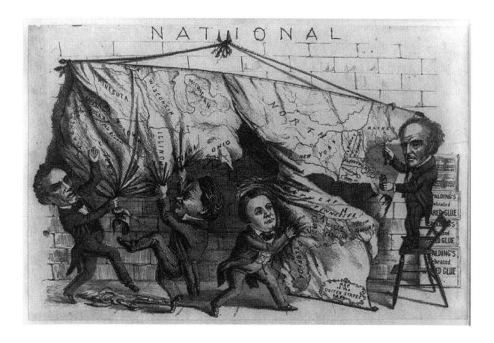

South Carolina didn't intend to secede by itself; they were going to have support from their Sister States on this one. They were not going to try to wing something this encompassing alone as it had with the Nullification Crisis. It sent ambassadors to other Southern States. Soon, six more States of the Deep South—Mississippi, Florida, Alabama, Georgia, Louisiana and Texas, in that order—renounced their compact with the United States. Initially, 7 out of the 33 states were leaving this country; Lincoln caused almost one third of the nation to quit.

"The tea has been thrown overboard, the revolution of 1860 has been initiated."

THE CHARLESTON MERCURY

CHARLESTON

MERCURY

EXTRA:

Passed unanimously at 1.15 o'clock, P. M., December 20th, 1860.

AN ORDINANCE

To dissolve the Union between the State of South Carolina and other States united with her under the compact entitled " The Constitution of the United States of America."

We, the People of the State of South Carolina, in Convention assembled, do declare and ordain, and it is hereby declared and ordained,

That the Ordinance adopted by us in Convention, on the twenty-third day of May, in the year of our Lord one thousand seven hundred and eighty-eight, whereby the Constitution of the United States of America was ratified, and also, all Acts and parts of Acts of the General Assembly of this State, ratifying amendments of the said Constitution, are hereby repealed; and that the union now subsisting between South Carolina and other States, under the name of " The United States of America," is hereby dissolved.

THE

UNION

IS

DISSOLVED!

"We, the people of the State of South Carolina, in convention assembled, do declare and ordain, and it is hereby declared and ordained, That(sic) the ordinance adopted by us in convention on the twenty-third day of May, in the year of our Lord one thousand seven hundred and eighty-eight, whereby the Constitution of the United States of America was ratified, and also all acts and parts of acts of the General Assembly of this State ratifying amendments of the said Constitution, are hereby repealed; and that the union now subsisting between South Carolina and other States, under the name of the 'United States of America,' is hereby dissolved."

Done at Charleston the twentieth day of December, in the year of our Lord one thousand eight hundred and sixty.

NO LONGER A BLUFF

Before April 1861, Northerners did not take the Southern secession seriously. Secession was, by birth, a Northern child. As I said, it was New England, itself, that started this secession parade. No State had done it before, and the nation was stunned.

The act of secession lies deep within the American psyche. When the 13 colonies rebelled against Great Britain in the War for American Independence, it was an act of secession, one that is, again, celebrated by Americans to this day. We were children of secession, and the nut never falls far from the tree.

By early 1861, six States had gathered in Montgomery, Alabama; Texas would join them soon. Montgomery, Alabama was chosen as the seat of a new government. During this process, committees were chosen, a Provisional Constitution was drafted, approved, and an election of a Provisional President was held. The office of Provisional President fell into the hands of Mississippi Senator Jefferson Finis Davis.

Jefferson Davis was a leading Southern politician, and held the great respect of most of his contemporaries. There were those among the Southern delegates who opposed Davis' election, and some of those opponents will, at a later time, create roadblocks in the handling of Southern affairs. Davis was a capable leader, and began immediately to organize his Cabinet, as well as establishing the mechanism for a National Government.

Secession was a much more complex situation than one might think. Those who sought disunion in the wake of the election of 1860 believed fervently that the survival of the Southern honor, wealth, and regional character was at stake.

In the rhetoric of secession, then, it is not surprising to find outright assertions of the rightness of slavery. As Confederate Vice President Alexander Stephens boldly phrased it, "Our new government is founded upon. . . the great truth that the negro(sic) is not equal to the white man; that slavery-- subordination to the superior race-- is his natural and normal condition. This, our new government, is the first in the history of the world based upon this great physical, philosophical, and moral truth."

(Please compare, again, the words of Lincoln: September 18, 1858, Lincoln made his position clear. "I will say then that I am not, nor ever have been, in favor of bringing about in any way the social and political equality of the white and black races.")

Also, keep in mind some quotes from the Christian Bible of that time, The King James Version, allowed this institution to thrive in the deeply religious Christian South:

BIBLICAL QUOTES ON SLAVERY

Leviticus 25:44-46 ... "As for your male and female slaves whom you may have: you may buy male and female slaves from among the nations that are around you. You may also buy from among the strangers who sojourn with you and their clans that are with you, who have been born in your land, and they may be your property. You may bequeath them to your sons after you to inherit as a possession forever. You may make slaves of them, but over your brothers the people of Israel you shall not rule, one over another ruthlessly."

Ephesians: 6:5... "Slaves, obey your earthly masters with fear and trembling, with a sincere heart, as you would Christ."

Joel: 3:8 "... will sell your sons and your daughters into the hands of the people of Judah, and they will sell them to the Sabeans, to a nation far away, for the Lord has spoken."

Colossians: 3:2... "Slaves, obey in everything those who are your earthly masters, not by way of eye-service, as people-pleasers, but with sincerity of heart, fearing the Lord."

Titus: 9-10... "Slaves are to be submissive to their own masters in everything; they are to be well-pleasing, not argumentative, not pilfering, but showing all good faith, so that in everything they may adorn the doctrine of God our Savior."

And here is the kicker. This verse allows Christians to keep slaves....it is in the Bible. Look it up, if you haven't seen it. King James Version:

1 Timothy: 6:1-2... "Let as many servants as are under the yoke count their own masters worthy of all honor, that the name of God and his doctrine be not blasphemed. ²And they that have believing masters, let them not despise them, because they are brethren; but rather do them service, because they are faithful and beloved, partakers of the benefit. These things teach and exhort." (Christian slaves and their Christian masters? It looks that way to many who read this... makes you think a little harder.)

Does this really imply Christians holding Christians slave? "Believing" masters, their "brethren". All of this was interpreted as Christians having slaves with God's blessing.

I hope you can begin to see the confusion in the scripture, not to mention the argument over what it meant.

One can pull from this great Book many angles on such subjects. The Northern Churches quoted these verses from the same Book:

Galatians: 5:1... "Stand fast therefore in the liberty wherewith Christ hath made us free, and be not entangled again with the yoke of bondage."

Galatians: 3:28 "There is neither Jew nor Greek, there is neither slave nor free, there is no male and female, for you are all one in Christ Jesus."

That verse can be taken either way.

When you look closely at all of the verses in the Bible, the majority does uphold slavery and details the punishment for slaves, even in the New Testament. And so it goes. Different Christians, different back grounds in their beliefs, and it was all coming to a head.

Read this quote from Jefferson Davis:

"Let the gentleman go to Revelation to learn the decree of God, let him go to the Bible...I said that slavery was sanctioned in the Bible, authorized, regulated, and recognized from Genesis to Revelation...Slavery existed then in the earliest ages, and among the chosen people of God; and in Revelation we are told that it shall exist till the end of time shall come."

In Lincoln's first inaugural address, Lincoln performed a delicate balancing act designed to warn the South against persisting in its course and to reassure it that slavery would not be fully abolished. "If the minority will not acquiesce", he said, "the majority must, or the government must cease. There is no other alternative; for continuing the government, is acquiescence on one side or the other". He also mentioned an amendment that would guarantee slavery in the United States forever.

As events would show, neither side was in the mood to acquiesce. With the intensification of rhetorical bluster and the erosion of a middle ground where compromise was possible, the country slid toward war.

It is at this point in time that our social history takes over from truth. Abraham Lincoln did, indeed, draft and issue the Emancipation Proclamation. He is often given credit for almost single-handedly freeing the slaves. That is how most will remember this time in our history....but.....

THE CORWIN AMENDMENT

Let us examine the other side of Mr. Lincoln, and fill in the blanks. Abraham Lincoln was always a public advocate for the ending of slavery, but, as we have already said, his primary objective was the preservation of the Union, whatever the costs. Later in this book, I will have quotes and photos of the primary figures in this story.

It is a fact that Abraham Lincoln did act to preserve slavery in this nation forever just three days after he was inaugurated.

OHIO REPRESENTATIVE THOMAS CORWIN

"No amendment shall be made to the Constitution which will authorize or give to Congress power to abolish or interfere, within any State, with the domestic institutions thereof, including that of persons held to labor or service by the laws of said State."

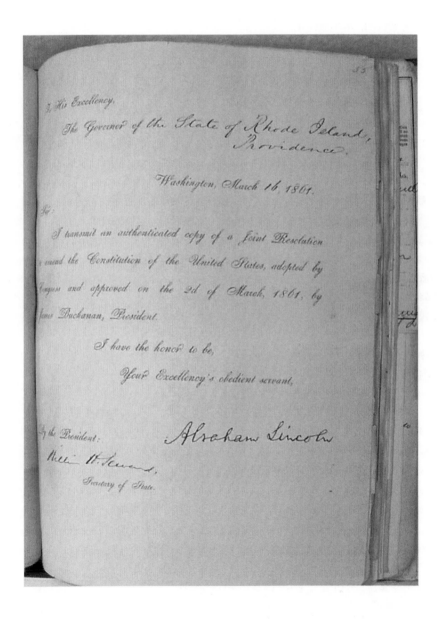

TEXT FROM JAMES BUCHANNAN'S LETTER
SIGNED BY ABRAHAM LINCOLN

"I transmit an authenticated copy of the Joint Resolution to amend the Constitution of the United States, adopted by Congress and approved on the 2d(sic) of March, 1861, by James Buchanan, President.
I have the honor to be,
Your (sic) Excellency's obedient servant,
Abraham Lincoln"

The Corwin Amendment would have made slavery constitutional and permanent, and Lincoln endorsed it, plain and simple.

Despite the latest fiction out of Hollywood, the movie *"LINCOLN"*, there is no evidence that Lincoln provided any significant assistance in the passage of the Thirteenth Amendment in the House of Representatives in 1865. There *is* evidence of his effectiveness in getting an earlier Thirteenth Amendment, (The Corwin Amendment), through the *House and the Senate in 1861*. The Corwin Amendment had passed both the Republican-controlled House and the Republican-dominated U.S. Senate on March 2, 1861, two days before Lincoln's inauguration. This pro-slavery amendment was sent to the states for ratification by Lincoln himself. The letter is above; read it yourself, again. It is the "smoking gun", so to speak.

This early version of the 13th Amendment was introduced into the Senate by William Seward, a Senator from New York. Seward, as we said, was made Lincoln's Secretary of State.

The Corwin Amendment was an effort to stall and pacify the South as well as quash the secessionist movement. It proposed to do three things.

First: To protect slavery by giving each State the power to regulate the "domestic institutions" within its borders. This was an enticing carrot for the slave states; stay in the Union and you can keep slavery.

Second: To dispossess Congress of the power to "abolish or interfere" with slavery.

Third: To make it unamendable (sic) by providing that "no amendment shall be made to the Constitution" that would undo the Corwin Amendment.

This was a permanent deal offered by the North, one that our school books just left out. This changes the complexion of the beginnings of the War as well as the real feelings that Northerners had toward the Africans. This little omission by our public schools, in an effort not to upset some folks, sets the tone of our current history; doing this, they withhold Black History.

Funny, isn't it, that we have "Black History Month," but we hide more than a hundred years of Black History from our African-American youth.

Our kids are not being told the truth, plain and simple.

The North decided, at some point, that their willingness to keep slavery forever certainly did not fit the image they wanted to present, so they just decided to omit it; an "Inconvenient Truth".

Lincoln's future Secretary of State, William H. Seward, had sponsored the Corwin Amendment in the Senate, and the newly-elected President, Lincoln, himself, defended the States' right to adopt it. In his first Inaugural Address, Lincoln declared that he had "no objection" to the Corwin Amendment, nor that it be made forever unamendable (sic).

His exact words were: "I understand a proposed amendment to the Constitution (The Corwin Amendment) – which amendment, however, I have not seen – has passed Congress to the effect that the Federal Government shall never interfere with the domestic institutions of the States, including that of persons held to service . . . . [H]olding (sic) such a provision to now be implied constitutional law, I have no objection to its being made express and irrevocable".

Lincoln's focus was on the Union, not freeing the slaves in early 1861. The Great Emancipator was a politician. That, in my mind, pretty well summed it up for me. You have to ask yourself, again, what side of his mouth was he talking out of? What was the South to believe? What "truth" was he using, and for what end?

The Corwin Amendment won two-thirds support in both the House and the Senate in early 1861. Ohio was the first state to ratify the amendment, and Maryland and Illinois followed suit, but the onset of the Civil War interrupted the states' ratification of the amendment. Had it been ratified, however, the Corwin Amendment would have become the 13th Amendment, forever protecting slavery instead of abolishing it; and the Amendment would have passed with the support of the man who issued the Emancipation Proclamation of 1863. Politicians... don't you just love them? This was the best soap opera ever played.

Although its ratification was disrupted by the Civil War, the Corwin Amendment is still, to this day, not actually dead. Oddly enough, it lies dormant, ready to be ratified by the required number of states. Somebody might tell the folks in Hollywood the real facts; you can always catch them at their day-spa, of course, sipping a frap-a-dap-frat latte', (or something), while pumping more of their belly-fat into their lips...

What if we decided to put this piece of filtered history back into our public school books? Can you imagine the upset and confusion of modern-day educators trying to undo all of the bias that our history books have created? Just because it is "writ", it doesn't make it true. We have a lot of rewriting to do to help get this time period right. Let's dig some more, shall we?

WILLIAM HENRY SEWARD

William Seward was an early opponent of slavery, and was a major player in the early formation of the new Republican Party. He was considered the front-runner for the Presidential election in 1860. After being just barely edged out by Abraham Lincoln at the Chicago Convention, Lincoln chose him to be his Secretary of State. Later on, when Seward tried to resign, Lincoln refused his resignation. Lincoln needed his opposition close.

Seward believed himself superior to Lincoln, and actually referred to him as a "Buffoon" at one point. Lincoln knew Seward to be crafty and intelligent and was impressed with his handling of the "Trent Affair". (This little bump in the road involved an American ship stopping a British ship near Cuba to remove two Confederate emissaries. England had yelled "Foul". The United States backed down, freed the Confederates, and with some slick talk, Seward had made everything O.K. with England, and saved face for the Lincoln Administration. Lincoln couldn't risk two wars going on at the same time.)

Seward was also known for some deceptive and devious moves, some that played a part in speeding up the onset of this war. Questions remain, on some points, did Lincoln have a greater role in the deception, or was it just Seward; so much cover-up.

Seward's arrogance can best be summed up with a comment that he made to Lord Byron, the English Ambassador to the United States. He told him that he (Seward) could have any man arrested, and did the Queen of England have that kind of power?

Seward was notorious for having a bell on his desk. When he rang it, a secretary would come in, pick up the piece of paper laying close by. The individual whose name that was on that piece of paper disappeared, was sent to prison without a trial, or was sent South. He had that little respect for the law; anything for the Union? Did the means justify the end? If you win, it does.

Looking at history books today, Seward is almost sainted for his role in Lincoln's administration.

Historians vilify Davis for upholding the Constitution and praise men like Seward. To the victors goes the history re-write.

CHAPTER SEVEN

CRITICAL TIME-LINE

This time-line is a summation of how events fell into place. Refer back to this often, if you need to.

Nov. 6, 1860... Abraham Lincoln wins election as 16th President of the United States with only 39.8% of the Popular Vote.

Nov. 8, 1860... Colonel John L. Gardner, commanding United States forces in Charleston Harbor, orders Captain Truman Seymour, of his command, to transfer arms from the Charleston Arsenal to Fort Moultrie. The shipment is blocked by Charleston civilians.

Nov. 15, 1860... Major Robert Anderson, of Kentucky, is ordered to assume command of the United States forces in Charleston Harbor, replacing Colonel Gardner.

MAJOR ROBERT ANDERSON, U.S.A.

Nov. 22, 1860... Major Anderson arrives in Charleston.

Nov. 23, 1860... Anderson requests reinforcements from the War Department.

Dec. 4, 1860... President Buchanan's Fourth Annual Message read to Congress.

Dec. 8, 1860... President Buchanan meets with four members of the South Carolina Congressional Delegation.

Dec. 11, 1860... Major Don Carlos Buell arrives in Charleston with verbal orders for Anderson. Buell makes a written memorandum of the verbal orders.

Dec 17, 1860... South Carolina Governor Francis Pickens requests permission of President Buchanan to send a garrison of no more than 25 men to Fort Sumter. Lieutenant J.G. Foster, of the Federal garrison, draws 40 muskets from the Federal Arsenal in Charleston.

GOVERNOR FRANCIS PICKENS, S.C.

Dec. 19, 1860... Foster is ordered by the Secretary of War, John Floyd, to return the muskets, which he does. Secretary of War Floyd orders 125 heavy cannon to be shipped from Pittsburgh to the incomplete fortifications in the Deep South.

Dec. 25, 1860... President Buchanan learns of Floyd's efforts to ship cannon to Southern forts, and countermands the orders.

Dec. 26, 1860... Major Anderson moves his command from Fort Moultrie to Fort Sumter.

Dec. 27, 1860... South Carolina Governor Pickens demands that Anderson return to Fort Moultrie; Anderson refuses. South Carolina troops occupy Fort Moultrie and Castle Pinckney.

Dec. 28, 1860... General Winfield Scott writes to President Buchanan, advocating the sending of reinforcements to Fort Sumter.

GENERAL WINFIELD SCOTT, U.S.A.

Dec. 29, 1860... Floyd resigns as Secretary of War.

Dec. 30, 1860... South Carolina seizes the Charleston Arsenal. General Scott, again, writes to Buchanan, urging the reinforcement of Fort Sumter.

Dec. 31, 1860... Postmaster-General Joseph Holt named Secretary of War, replacing Floyd. President Buchanan refuses to order Major Anderson back to Fort Moultrie, and instead issues orders to send reinforcements and provisions to him at Fort Sumter.

Jan. 2, 1861... South Carolina seizes Fort Johnson, in Charleston Harbor.

Jan. 5, 1861... *THE STAR OF THE WEST* sails from New York with 250 recruits and supplies for Fort Sumter on board.

THE STAR OF THE WEST

(Point of trivia: *THE STAR OF THE WEST* was captured later in the War near Indianola, Texas, and was moved to Greenwood, Mississippi. It was there that General Pemberton, C.S.A., ordered her stripped and sunk as a hindrance to the Yankee flotilla. She still lies next to the earth works of Ft. Pemberton in the Yazoo River.)

Jan. 7, 1861... The House of Representatives passes a resolution supporting Major Anderson's shift from Fort Moultrie to Fort Sumter.

Jan. 8, 1861... Secretary of the Interior, Jacob Thompson, the last Southerner in Buchanan's Cabinet, resigns, but not before he telegraphs South Carolina officials about the mission of *The Star of the West*.

Jan. 9, 1861... *THE STAR OF THE WEST* is fired upon by the Citadel Cadets as it enters Charleston Harbor, and is driven off. These are the first shots of anger fired in the War.

Jan. 11, 1861... South Carolina demands that Major Anderson surrender Fort Sumter; he refuses.

Jan. 13, 1861... J.W. Hayne, Commissioner from South Carolina to the United States, arrives in Washington to negotiate the status of Fort Sumter.

Jan. 14, 1861... Virginia's legislature calls for a secession convention.

Jan. 19, 1861... Virginia invites states to a convention in Washington to propose compromise measures aimed at solving the crisis. This leads to the so-called Washington Peace Conference.

Feb. 1, 1861... South Carolina's demand that Fort Sumter be turned over to the State is presented to President Buchanan by Commissioner Hayne.

Feb. 4, 1861... Washington Peace Conference opens. Virginia holds elections for delegates to her secession convention, with outright secessionists losing badly.

Feb. 6, 1861... Secretary of War Holt informs Hayne that under no circumstances will Fort Sumter be surrendered.

Feb. 8, 1861... The Provisional Constitution of the Confederate States of America is approved in Montgomery, Alabama. The next day, Jefferson Finis Davis, of Mississippi, would be elected as Provisional President, and Alexander Stephens, of Georgia, as Provisional Vice-President.

Feb. 9, 1861... Tennessee rejects a call for a secession convention by a vote of 68,000 to 59,500. *THE U.S.S. BROOKLYN* arrives at Fort Pickens, off of Pensacola, Florida, carrying reinforcements. She is met by Confederate forces and told not to off-load; they comply.

Feb. 11, 1861... Lincoln leaves Springfield, Illinois, for Washington, D.C.. He stops overnight in Indianapolis, where he speaks to a crowd outside his hotel.

Feb. 12, 1861... Lincoln travels to Cincinnati, where he speaks to a crowd at his hotel.

Feb. 13, 1861... Lincoln addresses the State Legislature in Columbus, Ohio. Virginia secession convention opens.

Feb. 14, 1861... Lincoln leaves Columbus for Pittsburgh; after giving a speech, he leaves for Cleveland.

Feb. 16, 1861... Lincoln leaves Cleveland for Buffalo, New York.

Feb. 18, 1861... Brigadier General David Twiggs surrenders the United States troops in Texas to the State authorities. Lincoln leaves Buffalo for Albany and makes a speech before the New York legislature.

Feb. 19, 1861... Lincoln leaves Albany for New York City.

Feb. 20, 1861... In a meeting with Mayor Fernando Wood of New York, Lincoln says, "There is nothing that can ever bring me willingly to consent to the destruction of this Union".

Feb. 21, 1861... The Lincoln party leaves New York for Philadelphia.

Feb. 22, 1861... Lincoln addresses Washington's Birthday Celebration at Independence Hall in Philadelphia; he then leaves for Harrisburg, where he learns of suspected threats against him in Baltimore.

Feb. 23, 1861... After an all-night train ride in secret, Lincoln arrives in Washington City.

Feb. 27, 1861... Final day of the Washington Peace Conference. Lincoln meets with delegation from the Peace Conference and offers to evacuate Fort Sumter if the Virginia secession convention adjourns. Confederate President Davis appoints three commissioners (Martin Crawford, John Forsyth, and A. B. Roman) to negotiate with the Federal government.

CONFEDERATE COMMISIONERS SENT TO MEET WITH LINCOLN

MARTIN CRAWFORD   JOHN FORSYTH   A.B. ROMAN

Feb. 28, 1861... North Carolina rejects a call for a secession convention.

March 1, 1861... Davis assigns Brigadier General P.G.T. Beauregard to the command of C.S. forces in Charleston Harbor.

GENERAL P.G.T. BEAUREGARD, C.S.A.

March 3, 1861... Beauregard arrives in Charleston. General Winfield Scott writes to Secretary of State (designate) William Seward that he does not think Fort Sumter can be relieved.

March 4, 1861... Abraham Lincoln sworn in as the 16th President of the United States; in his inauguration speech, he pledges "to hold, occupy, and possess the property and places belonging to the government, and to collect the duties and imposts." (He is referring to the monies collected from duties and tariffs that the Southern ports were bringing in.) Secretary of War Holt receives word from Major Anderson that, without 20,000 men in reinforcements, he cannot hold Fort Sumter; additionally, his supplies will not allow him to hold out for much longer than six weeks. This note is communicated to President Lincoln on March 5th; Governor Pickens of South Carolina telegraphs the Tredegar Iron Works in Richmond, Virginia: "Please send 400 shells for Dahlgren guns in addition to those already ordered."

March 8, 1861... The Confederate Commissioners, using California Senator William Gwin as an intermediary, sent a memo to Secretary of State Seward, proposing to delay action against Fort Sumter for 20 days in return for a promise that the existing military position would be preserved.

March 9, 1861... First meeting of Lincoln's Cabinet; the President asks General Scott's opinion as to how long Anderson can hold out, and whether or not Fort Sumter can be relieved. The consensus is that the fort should be evacuated.

March 11, 1861... General Scott replies to Lincoln, saying that Anderson had hard bread, rice, and flour for only 26 days, and salt meat for 48; and to relieve the fort it would take a force of 25,000 men, adding, "As a practical military question the time for succoring Fort Sumter with any means at hand had passed away nearly a month ago. Since then a surrender under assault or from starvation has been merely a question of time".

March 14, 1861... Associate Justice John Campbell, acting as intermediary between the Confederate Commissioners and Secretary of State Seward, tells Seward that hostilities might break out at any moment.

March 15, 1861...   Lincoln's Cabinet declines to support an expedition to relieve Fort Sumter; only Postmaster General Montgomery Blair is opposed to evacuation. Justice Campbell tells Commissioner Crawford that Sumter will be evacuated in five days. This directive came from Secretary of State Seward. There is still a question as to whether or not it came from Lincoln.

March 18, 1861... Confederate General Braxton Bragg, commanding at Pensacola, cuts off passage of supplies to Fort Pickens. The Arkansas secession convention votes 39 to 35 *against* secession, but then votes unanimously to put the secession question before the people of the state in an August referendum.

March 19, 1861... President Lincoln asks General Scott to send a "competent person" to Charleston in order to obtain "accurate information in regard to the command of Major Anderson in Fort Sumter." Scott selects Assistant Secretary of the Navy Gustavus Fox.

March 21, 1861... Fox visits Charleston and Fort Sumter, where Major Anderson tells him he can hold out until April 15, and that no relief effort could succeed.

March 22, 1861... Stephen Hurlbut and Ward Hill Lamon, two Illinois acquaintances of Lincoln, leave Washington for Charleston on a covert mission from Lincoln.

March 24-25, 1861... Hurlbut visits old friends in Charleston and talks at length with James Pettigrew, who considers himself the only Unionist remaining in Charleston. Lamon meets with Governor Pickens and is allowed out to Fort Sumter to see Major Anderson. Lamon gives the impression to everyone he meets that Fort Sumter is to be evacuated. The two men leave Charleston for the return trip on the evening of the 25th.

March 28, 1861... Lincoln's Cabinet, meeting informally after a state dinner, reverses itself, and decides to send a relief expedition to Charleston Harbor.

March 29, 1861... Lincoln orders a relief expedition for Fort Sumter (in Charleston) to be organized.

March 31, 1861... Lincoln orders a relief expedition for Fort Pickens (in Pensacola) to be organized.

April 1, 1861... Confederate General Beauregard telegraphs his government that his batteries would all be in place in a few days, and asks, "What instructions?"

April 4, 1861 (11:00 a.m.)... Lincoln meets with Virginia Unionist John Baldwin; allegedly, offers to evacuate Fort Sumter if Virginia's secession convention will adjourn. (The evidence on this matter is controversial.)

(Afternoon) The Virginia secession convention votes 89-45 *against* an ordinance of secession. Later in the day, Lincoln orders the relief expedition to Fort Sumter to go ahead.

April 6, 1861... Lincoln sends a special messenger to Governor Pickens of South Carolina, informing him of the mission of the relief expedition, and promising him that if no resistance is offered, no troops, arms or ammunition would be moved into the fort.

April 7, 1861... Beauregard cuts off Fort Sumter's mail and daily market supplies. Virginia Unionist John Minor Botts meets with Lincoln and learns of the April 4th proposal to John Baldwin; like the Baldwin meeting, this encounter is controversial.

April 9, 1861.... The Confederate Cabinet concurs with President Davis's order to General Beauregard that Fort Sumter should be reduced before the relief fleet arrives.

April 10, 1861... Confederate Secretary of War Leroy Pope Walker orders Beauregard to demand the evacuation of Fort Sumter, under threat of bombardment. The Sumter relief fleet begins to leave New York harbor.

April 11, 1861

(2:20 p.m.)... General Beauregard demands the evacuation of Fort Sumter.

(5:10, approx.)... Anderson refuses, but adds, "If you do not batter us to pieces, we will be starved out in a few days."Beauregard communicates this comment to the Confederate government and asks for instructions.

(9:10 p.m.)... Beauregard is instructed: "If Major Anderson will state the time at which, as indicated by him, he will evacuate, and agree that in the meantime he will not use his guns against us unless ours should be employed against Fort Sumter, then Fort Sumter should not be bombarded."

April 12, 1861

(12:45 a.m.)... Beauregard asks Anderson if he can comply with the demands of the Confederate government. Anderson offers to evacuate on April 15th at noon, but declines to promise not to use his guns in support of any operations under the United States flag. This is considered unsatisfactory.

(3:00 a.m.)... Elements of the relief fleet begin to gather outside Charleston Harbor.

(3:20 a.m.)... Anderson is informed that the Confederates will open fire in one hour.

(4:30 a.m.)... Confederate batteries open fire on Fort Sumter.

April 13, 1861

(9:00 a.m.)... Fire breaks out inside Fort Sumter and begins to threaten the magazine.

(2:30 p.m., approximately)... Major Anderson surrenders after a 34 hour bombardment.

April 14, 1861... During the surrender ceremonies, a cannon misfires, killing Federal Private Daniel Hough and mortally wounding Pvt. Edward Galloway; four others (Privates George Fielding, John Irwin, George Pinchard, and James Hayes) are wounded. These were the only casualties.

FORT SUMTER

(Point of trivia: Fort Sumter was utterly destroyed during the War. Literally millions of pounds of ordinance smashed its walls and buildings. At the end of the War, all that remained was a pile of undistinguishable rubble. The Fort was partially restored and re-fortified during our Spanish-American War. Visitors now see little of the original structure; and it is hard to imagine what it looked like. There is another Fort Sumter, of sorts, that is in perfect shape. It is in California, at The Presidio, near San Francisco. It was a built between 1853 and 1861 to protect the riches coming from the Gold strike and later, re-enforced for any invasion from a Confederate attack. The fort is similar to Fort Sumter in a lot of ways, and is open year-round for visitors.)

Here is the official report made by General Beauregard after the bombardment.

THE BOMBARDMENT OF FORT SUMTER

Most people in this country have never read this document. It is an incredible study of General Beauregard's character and the character of this Nation in 1861. Read it, just as it was written; I have not altered it, or changed the spelling.

OFFICIAL REPORT OF GENERAL P.G.T. BEAUREGARD, CSA HEADQUARTERS PROVISIONAL ARMY

Originally Published: May 12, 1861

CHARLESTON, S.C., April 27, 1861

Brig. Gen. Cooper, Adjutant General, U.S.A.:

SIR: I have the honor to submit the following detailed report of the bombardment and surrender of Fort Sumter, and the incidents connected therewith. Having completed my channel defence (sic) and batteries in the harbor, necessary for the reduction of Fort Sumter, I dispatched two of my Aids, 2:20 P.M., on Thursday the 11th of April, with a communication to Major Anderson, in command of the fortification, demanding its evacuation. I offered to transport himself and command to any port in the United States he might select, to allow him to more out of the fort with company arms and property, and all private property, and to salute his flag on lowering it. He refused to accede to the demand. As my Aids were about leaving, Major

135

Anderson remarked, that if we did not batter him to pieces he would be starved out in few days, or words to that effect.

This being reported to me by my Aids, on their return with his refusal at 5 10 P.M., I deemed it proper to telegraph the purport of his remark to the Secretary of War. I received by telegraph the following instructions at 9.10 P.M. -- "Do not desire needlessly to bombard Fort Sumter. If Major ANDERSON will state the time at which, as indicated by him, he will evacuate, and agree that in the meantime he will not use his guns against us, unless ours should be employed against Fort Sumter, you are authorized thus to avoid effusion of blood. If this or its equivalent be refused, reduce the fort as your judgment decides to be most practicable." At 11 P.M. I sent my Aids with a communication to Major ANDERSON, based upon the foregoing instructions. It was placed in his hands at 12.45 A.M., 12th inst. He expressed his willingness to evacuate the fort on Monday afternoon, if provided with the necessary means of transportation, and if he should not receive contradictory instructions from his Government or additional supplies. But he declined to agree not to open his guns upon us in the event of any hostile demonstration on our part against his flag. This reply, which was open and shown to my Aids, plainly indicated that if instructions should be received contrary to his purpose to evacuate, or if he should receive his supplies, or if the Confederate troops should fire on hostile troops of the United States, or upon transports bearing the United States flag, containing men, munitions, and supplies, designed for hostile operations against us, he would still feel himself bound to fire upon us and to hold possession of the fort. As, in consequence of a communication from the President of the United States to the Governor of South Carolina, we were in momentary expectation of an attempt to reinforce Fort Sumter, or of a descent upon our coast, to that end, from the United States fleet -- then lying off the entrance of the harbor -- it was manifestly an apparent necessity to reduce the fort as speedily as possible, and not to wait until the ships and the fort should unite in a combined attack upon us. Accordingly, my aids, carrying out my instructions, promptly refused to accede to the terms proposed by Major ANDERSON, and notified him in writing that our batteries would open upon Fort Sumter in an hour. This notification was given at 3:20 A.M. of Friday, the 12th inst. The signal shell was tired from Fort Johnson at 4:30 A.M. At about 5 o'clock the fire from our batteries became general. Fort Sumter did not open fire until 7 o'clock, when it commenced with a vigorous fire upon the Cumming's Point iron battery. The enemy next directed his fire upon the Enfilade Battery, on Sullivan's Island, constructed to sweep the parapet of Fort Sumter, to prevent the working of the barbette guns, and to dismount them. This was also the aim of the Floating Battery, the Dahlgren Battery, and the gun batteries at Cummings' Point. The enemy next opened fire on Fort Moultrie, between which and Fort Sumter a steady and almost constant fire was kept up throughout the day. These three points -Fort Moultrie, Cummings' Point and the end of Sullivan's Island, where the Floating Battery, Dahlgren Battery and the Enfilade Battery were placed -- were the points to which the enemy seemed almost to confine his attention, although he fired a number of shots at Caps BUTLER's Mortar Battery, situated in the east of Fort Moultrie, and a few at Capt. JAMES' Mortar Batteries, at Fort Johnson During the day (12th inst.) the fire of my batteries was kept up most spiritedly, the guns and mortars being worked in the coolest manner, preserving the prescribed intervals of firing. Towards evening it became evident that our fire was very effective, as the enemy was driven from his barbette guns, which he attempted to (sic) work in the morning, and his tire (19th century word defined as "A tier; a row or rank. This is the same word as tier, differently written.") was confined to his casemated guns, but in a less active manner than in the morning, and it was observed that several of his guns en barbette were disabled.

During the whole of Friday night our mortar batteries continued to throw shells, but, in obedience to orders, at longer intervals. The night was rainy and dark, and as it was confidently expected that the United States fleet would attempt to land troops upon the islands, or to throw men into Fort Sumter by means of boats, the greatest vigilance was observed at all our channel batteries, and by our troops on both Morris' and Sullivan's Islands. Early on Saturday morning all our batteries reopened upon Fort Sumter, which responded vigorously for a time, directing its fire specially against Fort Moultrie. About 8 o'clock A.M., smoke was seen issuing from the quarters of Fort Sumter; upon this the fire of our batteries was increased, as a matter of course, for the purpose of bringing the enemy to terms as speedily as possible, inasmuch as his flag was still floating defiantly above him. Fort Sumter continued to fire from time to time, but at long and irregular intervals, amid the dense smoke, flying shot and bursting shells Our brave troops, carried away by their naturally generous impulses, mounted the different batteries, and at every discharge from the fort cheered the garrison for its pluck and gallantry, and hooted the fleet lying inactive just outside the bar. About 1 1/2 P.M., it being reported to me that the flag was down, (it afterwards appeared that the flag-staff had been shot away,) and the conflagration, from the large volume of smoke, being apparently on the increase, I sent three of my Aids with a message to Major ANDERSON, to the effect that seeing his flag no longer living, his quarters in names, and supposing him to be in distress, I desired to offer him any assistance he might stand in need of Before my aids reached the fort the United States flag was displayed on the parapets, but remained there only a short time, when it was hauled down, and a white flag substituted in its place. When the United States flag first disappeared, the firing from our batteries almost entirely ceased, but reopened with increased vigor when it reappeared on the parapet, and was continued until the white flag was raised when it ceased entirely. Upon the arrival of my Aids at Fort Sumter, they delivered their message to Major ANDERSON, who replied that he thanked me for my offer, but desired no assistance. Just previous to their arrival, Col. WIGFALL, one of my Aids, who had been detached for special duty on Morris' Island, had, by order of Brigadier-General SIMONS, crossed over from Fort Sumter to Cummings' Point in an open boat, with Private WILLIAM GOURPIN YOUNG, amidst a heavy fire of shot and shell, for the purpose of ascertaining from

Major ANDERSON whether his intention was to surrender, his flag being down and his quarters in flames. On reaching the fort, the Colonel had an interview with Major ANDERSON, the result of which was, that Major ANDERSON understood him as offering the same conditions on the part of Gen. BEAUREGARD as had been tendered him on the 11th inst., while Col. WIGFALL's impression was that Major ANDERTON unconditionally surrendered, trusting to the generosity of Gen. BEAUREGARD to offer such terms as would be honorable and acceptable to both parties; meanwhile, before these circumstances were reported to me, and in fact soon after the Aids whom I had dispatched with the offer of assistance had set out on their mission, hearing that a white flag was living over the fort, I sent Major JONES, the chief of my Staff, and some other Aids, with substantially the same propositions I had submitted to Major ANDERSON on the 11th inst., with the exception of the privilege of saluting his flag. The Major (ANDERSON) replied, "It would be exceedingly gratifying to him, as well as to his command, to be permitted to salute their flag, having so gallantly defended the fort, under such trying circumstances, and hoped that Gen. BEAUREGARD would not refuse it, as such a privilege was not unusual." He further said, "He would not urge the point, but would prefer to refer the matter again to Gen. BEAUREGARD." The point was, therefore, left open until the matter was submitted to me. Previous to the return of Major JONES, I sent a fire engine, under Mr. H. NATHAN, Chief of the Fire Department, and Surgeon-General GIBBES, of South Carolina, with several of my Aids, to offer further assistance to the garrison of Fort Sumter, which was declined. [???] cheerfully agreed to allow the salute, as an honorable testimony to the gallantry and fortitude with which Major ANDERSON and his command had defended their post, and I informed Major ANDERSON of my decision about halfpast (sic) seven o'clock, through Major JONES, my chief of staff. The arrangements being completed, Major ANDERSON embarked with his command, on the transport prepared to convey him to the United States fleet, still lying outside the bar, and our troops immediately garrisoned the fort, and before sunset the flag of the Confederate States floated over Sumter.

(Point of trivia: Beauregard and Anderson were very close friends going back to the early days when "Cadet" Beauregard was taught artillery by Anderson at The United States Military Academy (West Point). Anderson had been very impressed with his student and took him under his wing. He aided Beauregard in getting him various positions which speeded up Beauregard's rise in the military.)

Beauregard was hesitant about shooting at his friend, but was assured by Anderson that he would make it through long enough so that each man could say that they had done their duty. They were each men of honor, and took their oaths very seriously.

Sadly enough, though, there are no records of the two meeting after the War. Anderson traveled to Europe, and Beauregard made a fortune in Louisiana.

CONFEDERATE FIRST NATIONAL FLAG RAISED AT FT. SUMTER

CHAPTER EIGHT

AFTER THE SMOKE CLEARED

After the firing on Fort Sumter on April 12, 1861, President Lincoln called for 75,000 "volunteers" to "put down the rebellion". This action caused four more Southern states to secede. These four states, Virginia, Arkansas, North Carolina and Tennessee, declared that Lincoln had exceeded his Constitutional powers by not waiting for Congress to act, (as President Andrew Jackson had done during the Nullification Incident), and they were not going take up arms against their sister States. The Southern States did not look at this affair as a "rebellion", rather two countries at odds and coming to blows, if need be.

They had voted to quit (or secede from) the Union in the same manner that they had used to join the Union. They were not in violation of any international law as far as they had determined; they declared their independence the same way their forefathers had with England on the 4th of July, 1776.

This was no "Civil War".

A "Civil War" is defined as: "A war between factions or regions of the same country." The Southerners were no longer tied to the United States. They were not part of that country; they had just quit. TWO countries fighting each other is not a "Civil War".

The United States Constitution offers no instructions OR opposition to any State's leaving. Our Founding Fathers had not addressed the issue in a clear enough way for anyone of this time to know what was legal, and what was not. Our Constitution can be interpreted in a myriad of ways; that was the dilemma.

The Legislature of Tennessee, the 10th State to leave the Union, waived any opinion as to "the abstract doctrine of secession", but asserted "the right, as a free and independent people, to alter, reform or abolish our form of government, in such manner as we think proper". (Hark back to the words in the Declaration of Independence. What was the difference? There was none, plain and simple.)

In addition to those States that seceded, other areas of the country threatened to, as well. The southern portions of Northern states bordering the Ohio River held pro-Southern and pro-Slavery sentiments, and there was talk within those regions of seceding and casting their lot with the South. Illinois and Indiana provided nearly 10,000 combat troops for the South, total. Blacksmiths in Southern Illinois broke the horns off of their anvils as a silent protest against Mr. Lincoln's Army. Anyone today, from Illinois, knows that there is "Chicago" and then there is the rest of Illinois. Politically, Illinois has always been divided by region, just as other states still are due to their early formations.

A portion of Virginia did secede from the Old Dominion and formed the Union-loyal State of West Virginia. Its creation and admittance to the Union raised many constitutional questions— Lincoln's cabinet split 50–50 on the legality and expediency of admitting the new State. Lincoln wrote, "It is said that the admission of West-Virginia is secession, and tolerated only because it is our secession. Well, if we call it by that name, there is still difference enough between secession against the constitution, and secession in favor of the constitution." Mr. Lincoln had a high opinion of himself, to be sure.

Technically, West Virginia did not secede legally from Virginia at all. Its very birth in Wheeling was a farce in the eyes of the State Constitution. The folks in that area wanted nothing to do with Virginia's secession; to this day, folks in West Virginia will correct you and say that their State isn't "West Virginia"; it's "West-By-The-Grace-of-God-Virginia". The convention held in Wheeling that brought about their split is full of false and conflicting arguments. Still, the western part of Virginia always had their own path, and this war gave them the opportunity to take it.

Along this same train of thought, here is another piece of history that was glossed over by the North.

In today's school books, our American students are told that there was a total of 11 Confederate States, and there is no mention of Territories. Well, here you go; some more stuff that they didn't tell you:

THIRTEEN STATES AND TWO TERRITORIES

The Confederate States admitted 13 States and 2 Territories into the Confederacy; the Indian Territory and Arizona were also admitted into the new Confederacy. Who does one believe? Mr. Lincoln won the War, and he claimed there were 11 states. The Confederate Government admitted Missouri (October 31, 1861) and Kentucky (Nov 20, 1861), into the Confederacy by acts of their Congress. Our schools teach the number to be 11. Really?

One has to ask this question, "What 'politically-correct' school system is going to allow any teacher to reference a Confederate Book"? Our educational system has been so corrupted by special-interest groups, that we are not allowed honest history or discourse. Clearly, the Southern side has been erased all together.

Can you imagine the furor that would erupt in our Nation, after Election Day, if the Democrat or Republican votes were just not "counted"? What if one side or the other decided it was "politically incorrect" to recognize votes that did not fit the current Press's view of how things should be.

As ludicrous as this may sound to some, others feel that this was exactly the way Southern sympathizers were treated by the Northern Press and the National Government in 1865. They were "politically incorrect", and they had no vote. They did not count.

Citizens of this great Nation were just ignored and vilified in American History because someone did not like their politics.

Consider this point for a minute: these States and their voters were American; they had a right to vote. They had a right to be heard. They were willing to fight and die, if necessary, to maintain that right. Where are their voices in today's books?

ARIZONA ORDINANCE OF SECESSION

This ordinance was passed by the People of Arizona in Convention assembled at La Mesilla, Arizona Territory, on March 16, 1861. It was a full-blown and legal vote by their citizens.

The Territory of Arizona was a territory claimed by the Confederate States of America during The War Between the States. It consisted of the portion of the New Mexico Territory south of the 34th parallel north, including parts of the modern states of New Mexico and Arizona. Its capital was Mesilla, along the southern border. The Confederate territory overlapped the Arizona Territory created by the Union government in 1863, but the physical geography differed in that the Confederate Arizona Territory was approximately the southern half of the pre-existing New Mexico Territory, while the Union Arizona Territory was approximately the western half of what had been New Mexico Territory.

The territory was officially declared on August 1, 1861, following the Confederate victory at the Battle of Mesilla. Confederate hold in the area was soon broken, however, after the Battle of Glorieta Pass, (near Santa Fe), which was the defining battle of the New Mexico Campaign. In July 1862, the government of the Confederate Territory of Arizona relocated to El Paso, Texas, where it remained for the duration of the war. The territory continued to be represented in the Confederate Congress and Confederate troops continued to fight under the Arizona banner until the war's end.

The historical markers are still there. Public schools completely overlook this piece of history, as well.

THE INDIAN TERRITORY (OKLAHOMA)

During The War Between the States, The Indian Territory, (currently the State of Oklahoma), served as an unorganized region set aside for Native American tribes of the Southeastern United States following the Indian Removal Act. This vast area was occupied by captured Native Americans who had been forced on a form of a "Death March" referred to today as "The Trail of Tears".

The area was the scene of numerous skirmishes and seven officially recognized battles involving Native American units allied with the Confederate States of America. Some Native Americans, loyal to the United States government, organized loosely against Confederate troops; there were no major battles of this type.

A total of 7,860 Native Americans participated in the Confederate Army, as both officers and enlisted men; they were mostly from the Five Civilized Tribes: the Cherokee, Chickasaw, Choctaw, Creek, and Seminole Nations. The Union did not incorporate Native Americans into its regular army.

LAST SURRENDER BY A CONFEDERATE GENERAL

GENERAL STAND WAITE, C.S.A.

Despite popular belief, and the folks in Hollywood, Lee's surrender at Appomattox Courthouse was not the end of the War. Lee was only surrendering the part of the Army that he controlled which was The Army of Northern Virginia.

The final surrender of a Confederate General took place near Fort Towson in the Indian Territory (now abandoned).

This event marked the end of the Confederate Army's status as a combat element. The surrender took place on June 23, 1865 between elements of the Union Army and General Stand Waite, a Brigadier General and a full-blooded Cherokee Indian.

146

Most of the photographs one sees of this War are of White or Black soldiers. Most of the Blacks are in Union uniforms and the Confederate Blacks were just edited out. There were thousands of Native Americans and Hispanics as well as some Chinese Americans who were involved. Statistics indicate that most Hispanics fought Confederate.

COLONEL SANTOS BENAVIDES, C. S. A.

At least 2,500 Mexican Texans joined the Confederate Army. The most famous was Santos Benavides, who rose to command the Thirty-third Texas Cavalry as a colonel, and thus became the highest ranking Tejano to serve the Confederacy. Though it was ill-equipped, frequently without food, and forced to march across vast expanses of South Texas and northern Mexico, the Thirty-third was never defeated in battle. Colonel Benavides, along with his two brothers, Refugio and Cristóbal, who both became captains in the regiment, compiled a brilliant record of border defense, and were widely heralded as heroes throughout the Lone Star State.

RARE PHOTOS OF CHINESE-AMERICAN SOLDIERS

CONFEDERATE STATES OF AMERICA AND TERRITORIES

The above map indicates the Confederate claims to States and Territories. Our public schools teach that there were only 11 Confederate States and no territories. One has to assume that Mr. Lincoln didn't count anyone that didn't vote his way. Missouri and Kentucky are taught as "Border States", when, clearly, they had citizens who voted for the Confederacy. Are we to discount those Americans who do not vote the "accepted way"? It is something to consider the next time you read about "The Border States".

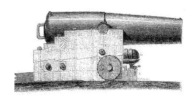

CHAPTER NINE

PEOPLE and QUOTES

JEFFERSON DAVIS

PRESIDENT OF THE CONFEDERATE STATES OF AMERICA

"Whether by the House or by the People, if an Abolitionist be chosen President of the United States, you will have presented to you the question of whether you will permit the government to pass into the hands of your avowed and implacable enemies... such a result would be a species of revolution by which the purposes of the Government would be destroyed and the observance of its mere forms entitled to no respect. In that event, in such manner as should be most expedient, I should deem it your duty to provide for your safety outside the Union of those who have shown the will, and would have acquired the power, to deprive you of your birthright and reduce you to worse than the Colonial dependence of your fathers."

....

" Slavery was established by decree of Almighty God...it is sanctioned in the Bible, in both Testaments, from Genesis to Revelation...it has existed in all ages, has been found among the people of the highest civilization, and in nations of the highest proficiency in the arts."

"The withdrawal of a State from a league has no revolutionary or insurrectionary characteristic. The government of the State remains unchanged as to all internal affairs. It is only its external or confederate relations that are altered. To term this action of a Sovereign a 'rebellion' is a gross abuse of language."

·························

"I will admit no bond that holds me to a party a day longer than I agree to its principles."

·························

"Truth crushed to earth is truth still and like a seed will rise again."

·························

"Neither current events nor history show that the majority rule, or ever did rule."

·························

"I worked night and day for twelve years to prevent the war, but I could not. The North was mad and blind, would not let us govern ourselves, and so the war came."

·························

"Never be haughty to the humble or humble to the haughty."

·························

"All we ask is to be let alone."

·························

"If the Confederacy fails, there should be written on its tombstone: 'Died of a Theory'."

ABRAHAM LINCOLN

PRESIDENT OF THE UNITED STATES OF AMERICA

"As commander in chief of the army and navy, in time of war, I suppose I have a right to take any measure which may best subdue the enemy."

....

"I believe this government cannot endure, permanently half slave and half free. I do not expect the Union to be dissolved — I do not expect the house to fall — but I do expect it will cease to be divided. It will become all one thing or all the other. A house divided against itself (sic) cannot stand."

....

"Any people anywhere, being inclined and having the power, have the right to rise up, and shake off the existing government, and form a new one that suits them better. This is a most valuable - a most sacred right - a right, which we hope and believe, is to liberate the world."

....

"We the people are the rightful masters of both Congress and the courts, not to overthrow the Constitution but to overthrow the men who pervert the Constitution."

"Better to remain silent and be thought a fool than to speak out and remove all doubt."

....

"You can fool all the people some of the time, and some of the people all the time, but you cannot fool all the people all the time."

....

"Those who deny freedom to others deserve it not for themselves."

....

"Whenever I hear anyone arguing for slavery, I feel a strong impulse to see it tried on him personally."

....

"I can see how it might be possible for a man to look down upon the earth and be an atheist, but I cannot conceive how a man could look up into the heavens and say there is no God."

....

"There are no bad pictures; that's just how your face looks sometimes."

LINCOLN AT GETTYSBURG

THE GETTYSBURG ADDRESS (unedited)

Gettysburg, Pennsylvania
November 19, 1863

Four score and seven years ago our fathers brought forth on this continent, a new nation, conceived in Liberty, and dedicated to the proposition that all men are created equal.

Now we are engaged in a great civil war, testing whether that nation, or any nation so conceived and so dedicated, can long endure. We are met on a great battle-field of that war. We have come to dedicate a portion of that field, as a final resting place for those who here gave their lives that that nation might live. It is altogether fitting and proper that we should do this.

But, in a larger sense, we cannot dedicate -- we cannot consecrate -- we cannot hallow this ground. The brave men, living and dead, who struggled here, have consecrated it, far above our poor power to add or detract. The world will little note, nor long remember what we say here, but it can never forget what they did here. It is for us the living, rather, to be dedicated here to the unfinished work which they who fought here have thus far so nobly advanced. It is rather for us to be here dedicated to the great task remaining before us -- that from these honored dead we take increased devotion to that cause for which they gave the last full measure of devotion -- that we here highly resolve that these dead shall not have died in vain -- that this nation, under God, shall have a new birth of freedom -- and that government of the people, by the people, for the people, shall not perish from the earth."

On November 19, 1863, President Abraham Lincoln delivered a two-minute speech at the site of the Battle of Gettysburg that was to become legendary. He had been invited by David Wills, a local citizen and judge, to make "a few appropriate remarks" at the consecration of the cemetery for the Union war dead. This last minute decision to invite Lincoln reflects the lack of stature the President of the United Stated had during this time. Mr. Wills also extended Lincoln a warm invitation to stay at his house. Lincoln accepted Wills' invitation only three weeks prior to the dedication, probably viewing it as an appropriate time to honor all of those who had given their lives in the War.

Edward Everett, the nation's foremost rhetorician, (speaker), of the day and principal speaker at the dedication, delivered a two-hour oration that caught the nation's news headlines. Lincoln's address was relegated to the inside pages of the paper.

Lincoln actually wrote five different versions of the speech. He wrote the first version in Washington City, and probably finished it in Gettysburg. He wrote the second version of the speech the evening before he delivered the address. He held the second version in his hand as he delivered the speech, but made several changes as he spoke. The most notable change was to add the phrase "under God" after the word "nation" in the last sentence. Lincoln wrote the final version of the address, the fifth written version, in 1864. This version also differed slightly from the speech he gave at the dedication of the cemetery, but it was the only copy he signed.

The story goes that after Edward Everett had delivered his speech and Lincoln got up to speak, there was a movement in the tired crowd. They were shifting about trying to recoup from the long-winded oration. The crowd had hardly settled back in when Lincoln finished his two minute speech. A lot of people never heard him speak at all. His voice was described as high-pitched and strained, (unlike the voice that Hollywood always portrayed), and he was not the dynamic presence we have come to create. He was almost a non-event.

After delivering the speech, Lincoln sat down. He later recanted that he thought the speech went terribly, and made a remark to that effect, and felt horrible about the whole affair.

A few days later, Lincoln received a letter from Edward Everett, the key-note speaker of the dedication at Gettysburg. Everett wrote Lincoln to say, "I should be glad if I could flatter myself that I came as near to the central idea of the occasion in two hours as you did in two minutes."

The speech will always be among the era's greatest. Southerners, needless to say, were not impressed.

GENERAL ROBERT E. LEE, C.S.A.

According to legend, when, not long after the war, a black man entered a Virginia church and knelt at the rail to receive communion, the first member of the all-white congregation to join him was Robert E. Lee.

....

"My chief concern is to try to be an(sic) humble, earnest Christian."

....

"I tremble for my country when I hear of confidence expressed in me. I know too well my weakness that our only hope is in God."

"This war is not about slavery."

....

"It is well that war is so terrible. We should grow too fond of it".

....

"Duty is the most sublime word in our language. Do your duty in all things. You cannot do more. You should never wish to do less."

....

"I like whiskey. I always did, and that is why I never drink it."

....

"We have fought this fight as long, and as well as we know how. We have been defeated. For us as a Christian people, there is now but one course to pursue. We must accept the situation."

....

"True patriotism sometimes requires of men to act exactly contrary, at one period, to that which it does at another, and the motive which impels them the desire to do right is precisely the same."

....

"Go home all you boys who fought with me and help build up the shattered fortunes of our old state."

....

"Madam, do not train up your children in hostility towards the United States Government. Remember that we are all one nation now. Dismiss from your mind all sectional hostility, and raise them up to be Americans."

ROBERT E. LEE ON HIS HORSE, TRAVELLER (sic)

(Point of trivia: When Lee purchased this horse for $200.00, its name was "Jeff Davis". Lee stated later that he could not, in good conscious, ride a horse named after the President. By the time he re-named it, he said that he was impressed with the horse's stamina and stride... ergo, the name "Traveller." (sic)

GENERAL ULYSSES S. GRANT, U.S.A.

"Leave the matter of religion to the family altar, the church, and the private school supported entirely by private contributions. Keep the church and state forever separate."

"Hold fast to the Bible. To the influence of this Book we are indebted for all the progress made in true civilization and to this we must look as our guide in the future."

··· ······························

"I know only two tunes: one of them is 'Yankee Doodle,' and the other isn't."

······································

"No other terms than unconditional and immediate surrender. I propose to move immediately upon your works."

······························ ··

"There never was a time when, in my opinion, some way could not be found to prevent the drawing of the sword."

······························ ···

"Although a soldier by profession, I have never felt any sort of fondness for war, and I have never advocated it, except as a means of peace."

······························ ····

President Johnson: "At what time can Lee and Beauregard and other leading Rebels be arrested and imprisoned?"

Grant: "Mr. President, so long as these men remain at home and observe the terms of their parole you never can do so. The Army of the United States stands between these men and you."

"The line between the Rebel and Union element in Georgetown was so marked that it led to divisions even in the churches. There were churches in that part of Ohio where treason was preached regularly, and where, to secure membership, hostility to the government, to the war and to the liberation of the slaves, was far more essential than a belief in the authenticity or credibility of the Bible. There were men in Georgetown who filled all the requirements for membership in these churches."

....

"The distant rear of an army engaged in battle is not the best place from which to judge correctly what is going on in front."

PORTRAIT OF A YOUNGER GRANT

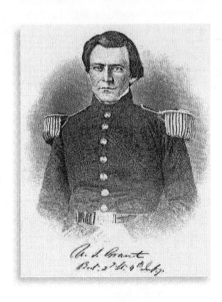

(Point of trivia: Ulysses Grant played women's roles on stage in California before the War. Army pay wasn't enough to get by on during the gold strike; Lee, on the other hand, never wore a dress.)

GENERAL THOMAS "STONEWALL" JACKSON, C.S.A.

"The patriot volunteer, fighting for country and his rights, makes the most reliable soldier on earth."

························

"Captain, my religious belief teaches me to feel as safe in battle as in bed. God has fixed the time for my death. I do not concern myself about that, but to be always ready, no matter when it may overtake me....That is the way all men should live, and then all would be equally brave."

························

"I am more afraid of alcohol than of all the bullets of the enemy."

························

"You may be whatever you resolve to be."

························

HIS LAST WORDS

"Let us cross over the river, and rest under the shade of the trees."

CHAPTER TEN

HISTORY OF THE CONFEDERATE FLAGS

Southerners revere their heritage and their history; they also have an almost unnatural affection and attachment to their flags. Mess with their flag, lose a limb.

I want you to really think about this, especially if you are not a Southerner: Southerners were at no time "Not Americans"… they were simply not "Northern Americans." There was a difference; there still is. Try to explain the word "Ya'll" to someone from New York City. Put some grits down in front of someone from Vermont and watch them ask to have the potatoes cooked some more.

People who may read this book, who are not from the South, cannot understand, nor fully appreciate, what a Southerner really is. We are not separate from this country; we are this country. We made this country. Our history proves it.

From the very early history of this nation, Southerners were always first to the aid of anyone in this nation in distress, even before we were a nation. Remember that the Southern Colonies sent aid, and men north during the pre-revolutionary times. A Southerner named George Washington was willing to spend thousands of his dollars to equip 1,000 men to come to the aid of Boston. We were always stepping up to help our sister colonies.

I suppose we can best be described as a "large family". We protect our own when others threaten, and we squabble among ourselves when we get too much face-time with each other.

Our love of our flag manifests itself as part of that protective impulse that we present when our Northern family members get pushy, or aggressive, or condescending with our part of the country. We also get testy when we can't find a decent glass of sweet tea in a Northern restaurant.

(Trivia point: The long teaspoon is actually a testing device for Southerners. When we travel abroad, say, to Iowa ,or overseas to Oregon, we have our server place the iced tea in front of us. We place our long spoon in the center of the glass and let it go... if that spoon moves any direction at all, there is not enough sugar in it.) Good Southern tea should be scooped, not sipped.

We are Southerners, first... and Americans, first.... and that is not contradictory to a real Southerner, it really isn't.

When Hollywood wants to take their shots at the South, they usually have some clever thing to say about cousins-marrying-cousins. They always play the Confederate Battle Flag card as a visual prop to introduce some element of the South that is the least attractive. These folks lack real creativity, in my opinion, and take the easy way out. When push comes to shove, folks, do you see a mass exodus of Southerners headed toward California?

OK, here is where we begin to open this can of worms and reveal who did what and why and when. I know that this part of the book is going to confuse everyone that ever got into a debate about "The Flag". I am not making this stuff up.

THE BONNIE BLUE FLAG

THE REPUBLIC OF WEST FLORIDA

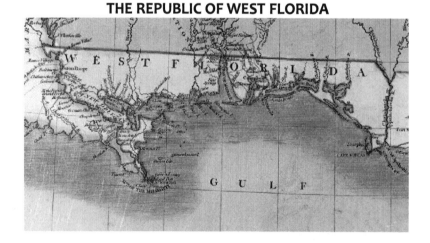

To begin at the beginning isn't as easy as it sounds. The history of flags associated with the Confederacy has to begin years earlier in Florida, of all places, during another up-rising.

There are tiny snippits of information that indicate, (without hard evidence), that a blue flag sporting a single star in the middle was used by troops during The Seminole Wars. It was not a wide-spread occurrence, but I have uncovered remarks in old writings that indicate that such a flag was used briefly during this time. I cannot verify this for a fact, but I mention it in case someone reading this book can fill in some blanks for all of us.

The most documented appearance of this flag happened in 1810, and it was associated with the small revolution that ended up creating The Republic of West Florida.

The area that we are discussing, known as West Florida, was originally claimed by Spain as part of what was called *La Florida*. It included most of what is now the southeastern United States. Spain made several attempts to conquer and colonize the area. Most of this action occurred during Tristán de Luna's short-lived settlement in 1559. Several permanent settlements developed during the latter part of the 17th century with the establishments of missions to the Appalachia. Pensacola was established in 1698 to thwart the French expansion into the area.

During this same period, the French established settlements in the region as part of "Louisiana". This included Mobile (1702) and Fort Toulouse (1717) in what is now the great State of Alabama. After years of back and forth "in your face" situations, it was finally determined that the Perdido River would be the boundary between French Louisiana and Spanish Florida. That river still separates the states of Mississippi and Alabama to this day.

In the treaty negotiations concluding the French and Indian War (Seven Years' War), France ceded to Britain the part of Louisiana east of the Mississippi River, notably excluding the Île d'Orléans, which includes New Orleans. A separate treaty transferred the rest of Louisiana to Spain. Spain ceded Florida to Britain in exchange for Cuba, which the British had captured during the war. As a result of these exchanges, the British controlled nearly the entire coast of the Gulf of Mexico east of the Mississippi. Most of the Spanish population left Florida, and its colonial government records were relocated to Havana, Cuba.

Finding this new territory way too big to govern as one unit, the British decided to divide it into two new colonies, West Florida and East Florida; these two areas were separated by the Apalachicola River. East Florida consisted of most of the formerly Spanish Florida, and retained the old Spanish capital of St. Augustine. West Florida comprised the land between the Mississippi and Apalachicola Rivers, with Pensacola designated as its capital. The northern boundary was arbitrarily set at the 31st parallel north.

Many English and Scots-Irish Americans moved to the territory at this time. The boys in London established an assembly, introducing democracy to the territory by 1766.

In 1764, the British had moved the northern boundary to the 32° 22′ north latitude, extending from the Yazoo to the Chattahoochee River, which included the Natchez District and the Tombigbee District. The appended area included approximately the lower half of the present states of Mississippi and Alabama. Many new settlers arrived in the wake of the British garrison, bringing with them a dedicated allegiance to their mother country (England).

In 1774, the First Continental Congress sent letters inviting West Florida to send delegates, but this proposal was declined as the inhabitants were overwhelmingly Loyalist. The colony was attacked in 1778 by the Willing Expedition and then overrun in 1779–81 by Spanish forces under Bernardo de Gálvez, culminating in the Siege of Pensacola.

In the 1783 Treaty of Paris, which ended the Revolutionary War, the British agreed to a boundary between the United States and West Florida at 31° north latitude between the Mississippi and Apalachicola Rivers. Britain also ceded both Florida provinces back to Spain, which continued to maintain them as separate colonies. However, the treaty did not specify the boundaries, sparking the West Florida Controversy. Spain claimed the expanded 1764 boundary, while the United States claimed that the boundary was at the 31st parallel. Negotiations in 1785–1786 between John Jay and Don Diego de Gardoqui failed to reach a satisfactory conclusion. The border was finally resolved in 1795 by the Treaty of San Lorenzo, in which Spain recognized the 31st parallel as the boundary.

In the secret Treaty of San Ildefonso of 1800, Spain returned Louisiana to France; however, the boundaries were not specified. After France sold the Louisiana Purchase to the United States in 1803, another boundary dispute erupted. The United States laid claim to the territory from the Perdido River to the Mississippi River, which the Americans believed had been a part of the old province of Louisiana when the French had ceded it in 1763. The Spanish insisted that they had administered that portion as the province of West Florida and that it was not part of the territory returned to France in 1800. The clearly illustrated the confusion, the bickering and the "you told me this" confrontations that arise out of such a confusing exchange of boundaries and obligations. You might want to read this again until you can firmly understand what is about to happen. This is why you get "clear title" on the next property you buy.

The United States and Spain held a bunch of exhausting and inconclusive negotiations on the status of West Florida. In the meantime, American settlers established a foothold in the area and resisted Spanish control. British settlers, who had remained, also resented Spanish rule, leading to a rebellion in 1810 and the establishment for exactly 90 days of the Republic of West Florida.

On September 23, 1810, after meetings beginning in June, rebels overcame the Spanish garrison at Baton Rouge and unfurled the flag of the new republic: a single white star on a blue field. This flag was made by Melissa Johnson, wife of Major Isaac Johnson, the commander of the West Florida Dragoons. It would later become known as the "Bonnie Blue Flag".

This piece of land was later annexed into the U.S. by James Madison... by force... on October 27, 1810.

(Point of trivia: What was known as "The Republic of West Florida" actually contained none of what is now Florida... but The Constitution of West Florida actually named itself "The State of Florida." So... today's Florida should actually be named "The State of Florida, Part Two, the sequel....got it?......)

THE BONNIE BLUE FLAG

THE CONFEDERATE CONNECTION

When the secession fever kicked in, Mississippi joined the fray with everything they had. They had dealt with the Federal government long enough, and the threat of being taxed out of business through the tariffs was the last straw.

Delegates gathered in Jackson on January 9, 1861, (the same day the Citadel cadets were firing on *THE STAR OF THE WEST*). They declared their independence from the United States, and drafted a document declaring themselves "The Republic of Mississippi"!!!

On that same day, they hoisted a blue flag with a single star above their capitol dome with great flourish and public mayhem. In that crowd, a man named Harry McCarthy got into the fever and was inspired to write new words to an old Irish melody called "The Irish Jaunting Car". He named his new song "The Bonnie Blue Flag", and premiered the song by the same name at a concert in Jackson, Mississippi later in the spring; it went viral. The flag became the symbol of the new secession movement, and the song "The Bonnie Blue Flag" was a hit. It became the second most popular song in the South, right behind "Dixie".

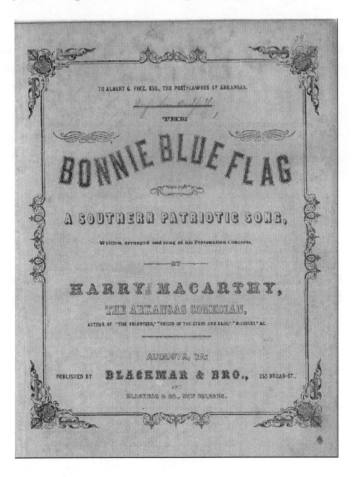

THE TEXAS CONNECTION

It had been that same flag that went west to Texas in 1836 during their struggle for freedom from Santa Ana and the Mexican government. After going through several changes, this flag ended up being placed vertically on the left with two stripes sewn on the right; white, above, red, below. This Third Republic of Texas flag design was later adopted by the Great State of Texas to represent the "The Lone Star State". (There had been another red flag with a single star that was introduced into Texas earlier in the 1800s. It may well have been the flag associated with the term "Lone Star State"...the connection with the blue flag has a closer link to the current Texas flag.) The irony was that "The Lone Star State" got their white star on a blue field from West Florida. I know that hurts you folks from Texas, but I didn't make this up, either. If it makes you feel any better, it was the same flag flown by the Confederate State of Texas, as well. It still is, technically, a "Confederate Flag". Ya'll never did change it after The War.

BIG RED

THE FIRST REAL REBEL FLAG

When South Carolina seceded from the United States on December 20, 1861, they became the Republic of South Carolina; there was no Confederacy, yet. The South Carolina Legislature broke into committees and began to structure their new Republic. It was decided at this point that South Carolina should adopt a new flag.

South Carolina's flag prior to this time had been a blue flag with a small crescent or "gorget" in the upper left quadrant.

A "gorget" was a device worn around the neck that served as neck-protection in battle and later reduced in size and adorned in a way that made them a symbol of rank in the military.

SOUTH CAROLINA REVOLUTIONARY WAR CAP

In 1775, Colonel William Moultrie was asked by the Revolutionary Council of Safety to design a flag for the South Carolina troops to use during the American Revolutionary War. Moultrie's design had the blue of the militia's uniforms and the crescent from the emblem on their caps.

This flag was flown in the defense of a new fortress on Sullivan's Island, when Moultrie faced off against a British fleet that hadn't lost a battle in a century.

In the 16 hour battle on June 28, 1776, the flag was shot down. Sergeant William Jasper ran out into the open, raised it and rallied the troops until it could be mounted again. This gesture was so heroic, saving Charleston from conquest, that the flag came to be the symbol of the Revolution, and liberty, in the state and the new nation.

It became popularly known as either the *"Moultrie Flag"* or the *"Liberty Flag"*. It soon became the standard of the South Carolina militia, and was presented in Charleston, by Major General Nathaniel Greene, when that city was liberated at the end of the Revolutionary War. Greene described it as having been the first American flag to fly over the South. (illus. 1)

The palmetto tree was added in 1861, (illus. 2), also a reference to Moultrie's defense of Sullivan Island; the fortress he'd constructed had survived largely because the palmetto trees, laid over sand walls, were able to withstand British cannons. This version, with the "Golden Palmetto" was adopted and flew only a couple of days.

This next simpler design ended up as the final flag used by The Republic of South Carolina; it still is the State's flag. (illus. 3)

The South had some support up North as well. The "Sovereignty Flag" (illus. 4) was raised over the Alumni Hall at Yale University by Southern sympathizers on January 20, 1861. It is also claimed that this was the first flag to be flown in South Carolina shortly after her secession on 20th December 1860.

After South Carolina seceded from the Union on December 20, 1860, a rush of Southern pride swept the City of Charleston. Getting caught up in the excitement was the military academy, The Citadel. The Citadel cadets designed and adopted their own flag, taking the new South Carolina Flag, and giving it a red background, hence the name "Big Red". (illus. 5)

The Citadel Cadets were manning a battery on Morris Island, just outside of Charleston harbor, in anticipation of an invasion or intrusion by Yankee ships. They knew that the Federal troops at Fort Sumter, Castle Pinckney and Fort Moultrie were running low of provisions, and they wanted no interference from the United States Government. On January 9, 1861, THE STAR OF THE WEST was spotted and the cadets opened fire across her decks; she promptly turned around and went home. "Big Red" was the first REAL REBEL FLAG....The first flag flown in anger against the U.S..

In 2007, Citadel alumni discovered a red palmetto flag in a museum of the State Historical Society of Iowa. It had been presented to the museum in 1919 by a soldier from the 20th Iowa Infantry. The flag matched descriptions of the flag that had been flown by the Citadel cadets; notable since red palmetto flags were atypical at the time. The curators knew of nothing at that time that could definitively link it to the cadets' Morris Island battery. Investigating the flag's provenance, members of the Citadel Alumni Association learned the Iowan soldier acquired it after the April 1865 capture of Ft. Blakely, Alabama, (near Mobile). The only South Carolina unit present was an artillery battery commanded by a Citadel graduate fighting with several men who had served on Morris Island or had other connections to the engagement. Unlike the Citadel Spirit Flag inspired by the mural or the state flag of South Carolina, the crescent on the Iowa banner faced inward. Although no eyewitness described the crescent in detail, alumni investigators found a February 1861 newspaper illustration showing the cadets flying a flag with the distinctive arrangement.

Although conclusive proof probably will likely never be found, the Citadel Historical Council and the Iowa Historical Society agreed that the evidence strongly suggests that the flag once flew over the Cadets' Morris Island battery. The State of Iowa Historical Society has loaned the flag to the school, where it is displayed in the Holliday Alumni Center. In 2009, the Citadel's Board of Visitors voted to adopt the original flag's design for the school Spirit Flag. God bless the Citadel and their honesty with our History. (Below, a Citadel button.)

"ANIMIS OPIBUSQUE PARATI"

PREPARED IN MIND AND RESCOURCES

THE CITADEL CADETS

FIRING ON *THE STAR OF THE WEST*

As the Southern States met to organize another nation, they chose Montgomery, Alabama as the site of the new capitol. There was serious consideration for naming the new nation, "New Washington", after George Washington. Southerners never felt alienated from their country's past and they embraced all that the South did to create and nurture our nation. They loved George Washington; he was a Southern boy.

George Washington was a Southerner, a Virginian, and they wanted to attach themselves more firmly to those colonial roots. As debates were engaged, the name "The Confederate States of America" was selected as a tribute and reaffirmation of the original Articles of Confederation, and what it stood for.

Southerners loved their colonial past and they knew that Southern men had set up a lion's share of the foundation of this nation. Thomas Jefferson wrote the bulk of the Declaration of Independence, James Madison had engineered the Constitution, and Patrick Henry had created the concept of a Bill of Rights. All three of these forefathers were Virginians, Southerners, and the South loved them for that.

In Montgomery, committees were selected and the Chairman of the Committee on the Flag and Seal was chosen. His name was William Porcher Miles, of South Carolina. Miles was a known "Firebrand" in his time. That term meant that he was constantly agitating for secession. He was a brilliant man, and sought the Presidency of the newly-forming nation.

WILLIAM PORCHER MILES

CREATOR OF THE FAMILIAR CONFEDERATE BATTLE FLAG

Without the support needed for President, he stepped back and accepted the Chair on the Committee on the Flag and Seal.

Under his direction, The Confederate Seal was finally adopted and included George Washington as the centerpiece with the five cash-crops adorning the edges. The term "Deo Vindice" was placed at the bottom of the Seal and, translated, it read, "God Will Vindicate".

THE GREAT SEAL OF THE CONFEDERACY

Miles made the selection of the flag an open contest. Using ads in various Southern newspapers, he solicited ideas and sketches from the Southern population and was able to gather close to 200 ideas via the mail at his offices in Montgomery.

The Committee on the Flag and Seal went to work. Miles had divided the designs into two categories: "ones that did not look like U.S. flags, and those that did". (That is his quote.)

The Committee reported that they had found "no suitable designs", but came out of their meeting with four designs for further consideration. Hanging the proto-types on a wall in a senatorial chamber in the Alabama Capitol building, the committee pondered some more.

Miles, at this point took the opportunity to present his personal design idea.

THE ORIGINAL *BATTLE FLAG* DESIGN

Miles presented his design in a verticle configuration. (see illustration) The Committee stated that it was "colorful, but looked like a pair of suspenders". That is a quote.

Miles was devastated. This familiar flag looked like this in its orignal conception...tell me that doesn't look like a pair of suspenders?! It did, it still does, and the Committee on the Flag and Seal said "no". It never was a National Confederate Flag.

There were many different Confederate flags, and most people in America are familiar with this one, alone. So much of our Southern History is tainted by rumors, legends, fairy tales and a lot of Hollywood goofiness. History.... altered by legend.

Make sure you look in the back of this book to see the illustrations that I have included. I made sure that I covered the basics for you.

One of the four flags that the Committee chose for consideration was a design by a Prussian immigrant named Nicola Marschall.

NICOLA MARSCHALL

Nicola Marschall was born in 1829 in the village of St. Wendel, in Prussia. He came to the United States in 1849. He arrived, first, in New Orleans, traveled to Mobile, and then Marion, Alabama. In Marion, he set up a studio, painting portraits and giving instructions in art and music. In 1851, he joined the faculty of the Judson Female Institute as an instructor of Arts and Language. Over the next five or six years, he developed quite a reputation as a portrait painter.

Realizing he needed further study, Marschall returned to Europe. There, he studied at the Duesseldorf Academy, and then in France and Italy. In 1859, he returned to Marion and re-opened his studio.

When the War began, Marschall was asked by Mrs. Napoleon Lockett and her daughter, Fannie Lockett-Moore, the daughter-in-law of the then Alabama Governor Andrew Barry Moore, to design a flag for the Confederacy. He drew three prototypes patterned after the flag of Austria. (illus. 6) The Committee settled on one of those designs. (illus. 7) The final version of that flag ended up with thirteen stars (13 Confederate States) before it was replaced in 1863. (illus. 8) Marschall was also credited for the main design of the Confederate uniform; it, too, was Prussian inspired.

There are stories that indicate that Marschall was inclined toward the old *Flag of 1776*, and that may have been part of the design, as well. The end result was known as *The Stars and Bars*. (Note: This is the REAL *Stars and Bars*). It was also referred to as *The First National Confederate Flag*.

(Point of trivia: The current Georgia State Flag is an adaptation of *The Stars and Bars*.)

The First National, or *"Stars and Bars"*, was used at the first major encounter of the War near the railroad junction near Manassas, Virginia.

This battle had two names: First Manassas or Bull Run. I suppose this, again, illustrates the nature of both sides in this conflict. Southerners had, and have, in my opinion, a more expressed religious leaning, as well as a closer tie to their communities. They named a lot of Battles after churches or communities, (e.g. Confederate name: Shiloh, after Shiloh Church).

The Northern folks named battles after geographic features such as creeks, mountains, and rivers, (Shiloh was referred to as Pittsburg Landing by the North; named after the landing close by on the river.) We couldn't even agree on where we were fighting, actually.

At the Battle of First Manassas, Confederate General P. G. T. Beauregard, who led the Southern forces, stated in his papers, that on top of the confusing mix of uniforms, his flag and the U.S. flag were too similar. At one point late in the battle, he delayed movement of some of his troops because he wasn't sure of their identity. He came close to calling up reserves to aid a full retreat, when he took a second look with his field glasses. A breeze lifted the colors of a Confederate unit just at the right moment, causing Beauregard to belay the order, and made his next advance. He stated later to a couple of officers that he would seek a "Battle Flag"... to better mark his boys.

According to his memoirs, he decided that the flag that an aide had brought with him might do the job. This staff member was the same William Porcher Miles that had headed the Committee on the Flag and Seal. Miles had joined up with his friend earlier at Charleston, just before the opening shots were fired.

Mile's flag had looked like a pair of "suspenders" to the Committee, but when turned horizontally, it did the trick. It sported the St. Andrew's Cross, and looked nothing like a U.S. flag; that is all it had to do. Later, General Joseph Johnston, C.S.A., his superior, agreed to the changes and adoption of a *Battle Flag*, and began his own modifications.

Johnston decided that the *Battle Flag* needed to look more military in its design, so he squared it up, and developed three sizes for the three branches, Infantry, Artillery, and Cavalry. The first *Battle Flag* was approved by the Confederate Flag Committee and was given a yellow bunting and displayed only 12 stars. (illus. 11) At that point, Missouri had been admitted into the Confederacy. Within days, Kentucky was admitted and the bunting was changed from yellow to orange. The flag displayed 13 stars. (illus. 12)

It wasn't long before the Colors changed again from the orange bunting to the now familiar white bunting. (illus. 13) The square version was the Colors for the Army of Northern Virginia, Lee's Army.

The long version of the flag came back into the War formally on May 1, 1863, when the Committee on Flag and Seal approved the full 13 star version of Mr. Mile's flag. This rectangle version was designated as the new *Confederate Naval Jack*. (illus.14) This new flag replaced the *First Confederate Naval Jack*. (illus.15) *The Naval Jack* flew on front of the ships then, as now, to identify the ship when it is in foreign ports. *The Naval Jack* saw a lot of use during the War, and is pictured in a number of period illustrations.

THE U.S.S MONITOR AND THE C.S.S.VIRGINIA

THE GREAT FIGHT BETWEEN THE "MERRIMAC" & "MONITOR", MARCH 9ᵗ 1862.

(Point of trivia: The illustration above shows the *Naval Jack* on the bow of the *C.S.S. VIRGINIA* and the real *Stars and Bars* on the stern. American history books in our schools call these two ships "THE MONITOR" and "THE MERRIMACK", as did this period engraving. This is a clear example of the refusal of the North to recognize real historical facts.

The truth is that "THE MERRIMACK" was burned to the waterline, re-surfaced by Confederate engineers, and re-built as an Iron Clad. She was re-commissioned "THE C.S.S. VIRGINIA". That was her name when she sank.

There were a number of Confederate ships that were captured and re-named by the North. Those names are still used. I feel it a bit hypocritical for the North to ignore the facts, and that our schools are still using this Northern gibberish. It was the "MONITOR and VIRGINIA", not the "MONITOR and MERRIMACK."

History, by a consensus vote, doesn't make it truth. Today, our boards of education vote on history; isn't that a bit strange? (I suppose that, in these days, one plus one equals six, if we vote for it......)

The continued confusion over the flags made it necessary for the Flag Committee to re-think the *Second National Flag*. By that time, the *Army of Northern Virginia Battle Flag* had seen a great deal of use and had developed a popular following. It was the inclusion of this flag with *The Second National Flag* that replaced *The First National Flag* on May 1, 1863. (illus. 9) This *Second National* became known as *Jackson's Flag* or *The Stainless Banner*. (General Stonewall Jackson's coffin was draped with the new National Flag in May of 1863.)

Again, the situation got worse when the Union Army and Navy were confused and misled by the new colors. *The Stainless Banner* had too much white, and led the North to think the Confederates were flying a surrender flag. There was talk that the Confederates were using tricks to get at the Union Navy by flying fake white flags. On the contrary, the Confederates felt slighted by this untrue allegation and a group of Confederate Naval officers petitioned the Committee to change the colors one more time. *The Third National Flag* (illus. 10) was adopted just weeks before the War ended. It was adopted on March 4, 1865. Very few of these flags were made and fewer were issued. This *Third National* was the last official flag of the Confederacy.

There were so many Confederate Flags used during the War that before it was over, Confederate General Joseph Johnston ordered the Army of Tennessee (in the Western Theater) to carry the *Confederate Naval Jack* as a *Battle Flag*. To make this all clear, the familiar Flag that everyone knows as the Confederate Flag was used as both a *Naval Jack* and *The Army of Tennessee Battle Flag.*

THE REST OF THE FLAG STORY

After the War was over, both sides organized Veterans Groups. The North organized "The Grand Army of the Republic" or the G.A.R.; the Confederate Veterans organized as "The United Confederate Veterans", the U.C.V.. The North chose the United States Flag, of course, and the South chose the square version of the *Battle Flag*. The crossed their Colors at those re-unions and there you have the final piece of the puzzle. (illus. 16)

CHAPTER ELEVEN

CIVIL WAR ODDITIES

As most of you have gathered by reading this book, I am not only interested, but driven, to do what I do. I love the research and the discovery. I have collected some strange stories about this time for this next section. It is a lighter side of this journey.

THE ORIGINAL SIAMESE TWINS

One case that amuses me is the story of the very unusual Bunker Brothers. Their names were Chang and Eng Bunker, and they are best known to some as "the original Siamese Twins".

They were natives of Siam, (modern Thailand), and joined at the sternum. They became a popular attraction with traveling museum exhibitions before the War and were able to save enough money to buy 110 acres in the Blue Ridge Mountains in 1839. They settled in that area of North Carolina and married sisters. They worked hard and built a successful farm with the use of slave labor. They became naturalized citizens and absolutely devoted Confederate sympathizers.

Union General Stoneman raided North Carolina in 1865 and wanted to draft some locals into the Union ranks, regardless of their political sympathies. There were 18 names of men over 18 that were placed in a lottery wheel. As it happened, Eng's name was drawn, but he resisted the draft, said he wanted nothing to do with the Yankees. Since Chang's name was not drawn, there was little General Stoneman could do; the brothers were not only joined at the sternum, their livers were fused. Stoneman had to let Eng go. Neither of the brothers served in the war; their eldest sons both enlisted and ended up fighting for the Confederacy.

Now you know where the term "Siamese Twins" was born; two die-hard Chinese Rebs.

MOURNING RITUALS

Wartime convention decreed that a woman mourn her child's death for one year, a brother's death for six months, and a husband's death for two and a half years. She progressed through prescribed stages of heavy, full, and half mourning, with gradually loosening requirements of dress and behavior. Mary Todd Lincoln remained in deep mourning for more than a year after her son Willie's death, dressing in black veils, black crepe and black jewelry. Flora Stuart, the widow of Confederate General J.E.B. Stuart, remained in heavy morning for 59 years after the 1864 death of her husband, wearing black until she died in 1923. By contrast, a widower was expected to mourn for only three months, simply by displaying black crepe on his hat or armband.

MOURNING WREATHS

Mourning wreaths were common in most Southern homes during this time. Hair was the most precious and personal thing you could offer or receive from a loved one. At the passing of one of the family members, a lock of hair was taken, treated, and woven into a wire form to form a beautiful wreath. It was open on the top as open hands reaching for God. One would pass by one of these wreathes today and mistake it for an arrangement of dried flowers.

Hair was also used in the construction of jewelry; many worn by women, while a great number of watch chains were made to be worn by a woman's loved one.

STONEWALL JACKSON'S ODD MOMENTS

Stonewall Jackson was a nut: he really was a little more than eccentric. I make no apology for my take on this fellow. As brilliant as he was, he was also way to the left of the "normal lane". The Confederate General thought himself "out of balance". Even under fire, he would raise an arm so blood might flow down his body and re-establish his equilibrium. (His hand was wounded when he did this during the First Battle of Manassas, (Bull Run). He refused to eat black pepper because it seemed to make his left leg weak; not the right leg, mind you, just the left. He was supposed to have sucked lemons, believing that they helped his "dyspepsia". He was most comfortable standing upright so that all of his organs were "naturally" aligned; he also ate that way because he said he would cramp up if he ate sitting down. He suffered from poor eyesight, which he tried to treat by dunking his head into a basin of cold water, eyes open. Stonewall would memorize entire chapters, while a professor at the Virginia Military Institute. His method of teaching was to simply recite by rote. Lord help the poor cadet that interrupted him mid-speech. He would be stared at, and have to listen to the entire speech again. Jackson had to mentally re-wind back to a spot where he could remember before he could complete his lecture.

He was brilliant, and to this day, The United States Military Academy, at West Point, uses a number of his cavalry tactics when teaching armored maneuvers. He once told a captain that he felt "as safe in battle as in bed".

He was a nut; a Southern nut, and I love him.

STONEWALL JACKSON

LINCOLN'S SPECIAL MOMENTS

Abraham Lincoln was assassinated on April 15, 1865. His leather wallet was found to contain a $5 Confederate bill, imprinted with the image of Confederate President Jefferson Davis. This did seem odd to some of those who attended, him I suppose. I have also read that Lincoln sat in Jefferson Davis' chair in the Confederate White House after Richmond had fallen. Lincoln may well have picked up the money there or in Richmond on that trip earlier in the month.

As many photographs as Lincoln had made, he never once was photographed with his wife Mary.

Abraham Lincoln's stovepipe hat was called his "desk and memorandum book" and also sometimes his "filing cabinet". This was because he kept mail, his bankbook, important papers, etc., in it.

Once, a shot was fired through Lincoln's hat (possibly by a hunter, but probably by a sniper) while the president was on horseback near the Soldiers' Home. The incident happened in August of 1864. The President asked that no mention of it be made to the public as it might worry his family.

Lincoln loved dogs and cats. One evening, during dinner in the White House, Lincoln was feeding one of his cats, Tabby, that was sitting in the chair beside him. Mary, his wife, urged him not to feed the animal at the table, and admonished him for using one of the White House's special pieces of gold-ware. Lincoln smiled and said, "If the gold fork was good enough for Buchanan, I think it is good enough for Tabby", and he continued to feed the cat throughout the meal.

At his second inauguration on March 4, 1865, President Abraham Lincoln wore a magnificent coat, specially crafted for him by Brooks Brothers. Hand-stitched into the coat's lining was an intricate design featuring an eagle and the inscription "One Country, One Destiny". Sadly, it was also this coat Lincoln was wearing when he was assassinated at Ford's Theatre (sic).

On October 3, 1863, President Lincoln made the traditional Thanksgiving celebration a nationwide holiday to be commemorated each year on the fourth Thursday of November. He did so at the urging of Sarah Josepha Hale. Her letters to Lincoln urged him to have the "day of our annual Thanksgiving made a National and fixed Union Festival". Perhaps Sarah is best known as the author of the poem *Mary Had a Little Lamb*.

One day, finding that the entire Cabinet was opposed to a proposal which he had made, Lincoln smiled and said, "The measure passes by a majority of one".

SOME MORE CURIOSITIES

Americans ate like our English ancestors for nearly 300 years. From the moment that our early cousins landed at Jamestown, we, as Americans, followed their example of eating with the fork in the left hand, upside down, and the broad eating knife in the right, sharper edge facing away. We ate like this for nearly 300 years. And then, a very strange and stupid idea was introduced, courtesy of the French.

About 1902, the French began promoting the idea that "eating with a knife in your hand was too aggressive". That is a quote.

These folks, we might remember, eat snails and cannot seem grow a decent mustache....just my own observation.

It became the rage during the latter part of the 19th century for the wealthy class in America to emulate everything French. Our wealthy class, taking their cue from the Parisians, laid their knives down, and people, like George Vanderbilt, pursued the idea that they wanted to be more continental, and less colonial. (George Vanderbilt was the fellow who built the 250 room "summer cottage" near Ashville, North Carolina....called Biltmore.)

Since most people are right–handed, and there was a recent vacancy created by this latest fad, the fork was shifted to the empty right hand, turned the other way so as to accommodate scooping; the left hand is banished under the table and out of the good graces of our wealthy class. (Nasty left hand, anyway, always staring at the right hand and nosing its thumb into that last pea left on the plate.)

As time passed, of course, the other social classes in America imitated the others above them, and now, everyone is doing the same goofy thing; that is why you eat the way you do.

After the hostilities and agitation erupted, Federal authorities imprisoned the Mayor of Baltimore, the Police Chief and a number of other Southern sympathizers, including the grandson of Francis Scott Key. This all occurred after Union troops were attacked while moving through Baltimore on their way to Washington City. Lincoln approved this action.

General Albert Sidney Johnston, a Texan by birth, commanded the U.S Army Department of the Pacific in California early in 1861. Refusing to join a Southern plot to capture the state, Johnston resigned his commission as soon as he learned that Texas had left the Union. He went to Los Angeles where he enlisted as a private with the Los Angeles Mounted Rifles, a pro-Southern volunteer unit that rode across Arizona and New Mexico to link up with Confederate forces in Texas. Johnston went on to become the second-highest-ranking Confederate officer, and was killed at the Battle of Shiloh. Pro-Confederate members of the Los Angeles County Mounted Sheriffs Deputies joined him in the trek east.

There was an attempt by Southern sympathizers to have California become part of the Confederacy. The furthest western skirmish took place just southwest of Stockton, California, after pro-Southerners took a public building and were chased out by Union supporters. The pro-Southerners had declared the State of California to be "The Pacific Republic"; didn't last long, however.

It was a Union General by the name of Lew Wallace, who later wrote the novel "Ben-Hur". He had earlier organized thousands of volunteers and militia for a defense of Cincinnati when the Confederate army threatened the city in September 1862.

Taking the risks of action from Confederate troops and guerrillas lurking close by, Union workers, in 1863, started building the Union Pacific railroad out of Kansas City, Missouri toward Lawrence, Kansas. America was expanding this great iron ribbon to the other end of the continent. This action extended the eastern segment of a transcontinental railroad that would connect in Utah six years later.

As part of the Confederate history of Arizona; Phoenix, Arizona was founded in 1865 by a former Confederate officer who had started farming there after Southern forces were chased out in 1862. He had tried to name the community "Stonewall", after Rebel General Stonewall Jackson, but was overruled by other settlers.

It was a Native American that surrendered last, you know. Cherokee Chief and leader, Stand Waite, a Brigadier in the Confederate Army, was the last Rebel general to surrender to Union forces in what is now Oklahoma. He gave up near the end of June 1865, more than two months after Confederate General Robert E. Lee surrendered at Appomattox. The location of that surrender is marked near the ruins of what had been Fort Towson in the Indian Territory.

Confederate cowboys were used in Florida and were dubbed the "Cow Cavalry." They were to round up and guard wild "scrub" cattle in southern Florida during the war. Their job was to provide beef for the Confederate forces. Their task was made difficult by constant skirmishing with Union forces that were landed in Florida by the blockade fleet.

Antiquities from the War with Mexico provided protection for Confederate forces near Corpus Christi, Texas during the War. Confederate forces kept a small Union fleet from capturing that port in 1862 by setting up cannons in earthworks built for the U.S. Army for the defense of Texas at the beginning of the Mexican War earlier in 1845.

Adam Johnson was able to capture a Federal arsenal at Newburg, Indiana by fooling the local militia into believing that he was about to blast them to pieces with a massive piece of Confederate artillery. That "massive piece of artillery" was a stove-pipe that his boys had laid across a wagon carriage and had been altered a bit to appear like the real thing at a distance.

A mere lad of 19 directed the artillery fire that saved Texas. One of the War's most striking victories was won by an Irishman in

Confederate service, Captain Richard W. Dowling, only nineteen, of the Davis Guards. With just 43 men armed with rifles and six small cannon, he defended Sabine Pass, Texas, in September, 1863, driving off a Federal fleet which tried to land about 15,000 men.

Dowling sank one gunboat, disabled and captured two others, and turned away the rest of the fleet.

He took 400 prisoners, all without the loss of man. This was the only command of record in the war to get its whole muster into official reports. All the men got silver medals from Jefferson Davis, the only such given by the Confederacy.

Firing on both sides was so inaccurate that soldiers joked that it took a "man's weight in lead to kill a single enemy" in battle. There was an estimate of 10,000 rounds fired for every man killed during this War. A Federal expert also interjected that each Rebel shot required "240 pounds of powder and 900 pounds of lead."

GENERAL JAMES W. RIPLEY, U.S.A.

It was a Union General who prolonged the War almost single-handedly. General James Ripley, the Ordinance Chief for the Union Army, repeatedly stalled the purchase and delivery of the most effective weapon that an army could employ. It was the Spencer repeating rifle that offered a huge advantage to the North at the beginning of the Conflict. Ripley believed that this rifle and the Henry rifle, another repeating rifle, were just "newfangled gimcracks".(sic) He hated all breech-loaders; to him, these "newfangled gimcracks" and were of no real benefit. He proposed that the troops would "shoot too much". He was worried that soldiers would simply waste ammunition. I think this is a good example of a "bean-counter" in the wrong job at the wrong time. Some things never change.

When it was all said and done, the Union Army ordered fewer than 60,000 Henry Rifles and fewer than 13,000 Spencers; compare these numbers to the more than 2,000,000 Springfields and Enfields used by the armies.

Elvis borrowed a Civil War tune written by Foulton and Fosdick, and made a hit with it in the movie "*Love Me Tender*". Another song called "*Tramp, Tramp, Tramp!*" became a church song titled "*Jesus Loves the Little Children*".

Early in the war, when a Confederate invasion of Washington was threatened, field guns were actually placed in hallways of the Capitol and Treasury Building. The iron plates, cast for the dome of the Capitol, were raised on heavy timbers between columns of the building as breastworks. Statuary and pictures were shielded with heavy planking, and an army kitchen was set up in the basement.

The Union Army had one company made up entirely of pugilists; there were others composed of musicians, farmers, or butchers. One temperance company went into battle stone sober, tradition has it. The 126th New York was the YMCA Regiment. Nicholas Busch, later Lieutenant Governor of Iowa, formed a woodchopper's corps of German immigrants who were unable to fight, (couldn't speak any English), and had them cut and haul wood for Mississippi River army steamers - pausing now and then to beat off guerilla attacks.

TWO-BARRELED GUN

One is OK, two would be better. In Georgia, a self-described weapons designer, John Gilleland, decided that firing just canister was too dangerous, not enough bang for the buck. Canister is a small tin or iron can, filled with large iron balls that are packed in sawdust. When fired, the balls came out like buck-shot, and caused a lot of damage. This was not the problem, seemingly; the problem was that the fellow decided the gun crew needed another shot. He went to work designing a "two barrel" gun.

The concept was simple: two barrels, two cannon balls with a long piece of chain attached to both. When the gun was fired, the two balls would come out, spread out, and the chain would somehow "mow" the opposing army down.

Here's the rub: the method for firing cannons at this time was by use of "friction primers". These "firecracker-like" tubes were full of gun powder and fulminate of mercury. They do not have absolute ignition reliability; one primer will most definitely ignite before the other; there was no way to make them ignite at exactly the same second. Result: one barrel goes off, pulls the other ball out of the other tube, and either spins around and kills the crew, or flies off toward an unknown direction endangering your boys in front. The story goes that it was fired once, and failed horribly. The balls came out, went out of control, plowed up a cornfield, killed a cow, and knocked down a chimney. Panic ensued, spectators ran over each other in the panic. The gun now sits in Athens, Georgia, (It is pointing north, unloaded, and safely out of the hands of the weapons engineer who probably coined the phrase, "Hey ya'll, watch this".) I love Southerners.

Before William Tecumseh Sherman became a great Union general, he was demoted for apparent "insanity". In October 1861, Sherman, then the commander of Union forces in Kentucky, told U.S. Secretary of War Simon Cameron he needed 60,000 men to defend his territory and 200,000 to go on the offensive. Cameron called Sherman's request "insane" and removed the general from command. In a letter to his brother, a devastated Sherman wrote, "I do think I should have committed suicide were it not for my children. I do not think that I can again be trusted with command". But in February 1862, Sherman was reassigned to Paducah, Kentucky, under Ulysses S. Grant, who saw not insanity but competence in Sherman. Later, when a civilian bad-mouthed Grant, Sherman defended his friend, saying, "General Grant is a great general. He stood by me when I was crazy, and I stood by him when he was drunk; and now, sir, we stand by each other always".

Both before and during the Civil War, Abraham Lincoln pushed to send freed slaves abroad. The policy, called "colonization", had been supported by Thomas Jefferson, James Madison, Andrew Jackson, Henry Clay—a hero of Lincoln's—and even Harriet Beecher Stowe, whose protagonists in "Uncle Tom's Cabin" ultimately emigrate from the United States to Africa. In August 1862, Lincoln brought five black ministers to the White House and told them that slavery and the war had demonstrated that it would be "better for us both, therefore, to be separated". He wanted to send freed blacks to Central America, even calling for a constitutional amendment authorizing Congress to pay for colonization. But, prominent abolitionists, such as Frederick Douglass and William Lloyd Garrison, were appalled by the idea. Lincoln never succeeded at gathering support for the policy; after he signed the Emancipation Proclamation, he never mentioned it publicly again.

Famous last words: during the opening stages of the Battle of Spotsylvania, Virginia, (May 8-22, 1864), Union Sixth Corps commander, Major General Sedgwick, tried to rally his men, who were ducking from Confederate sniper fire. The general started to say, "They couldn't hit an elephant at this distance", when a rebel sniper nailed him in the head and killed him instantly.

One of the South's most notable and outspoken post-war figures would have died at Sharpsburg on September 17, 1862, were it not for a hole in his hat. During the Maryland Battle of Sharpsburg, Confederate General John Brown Gordon was among the officers who led the defense of the Rebel center in the sunken lane. Shot in the face, Gordon pitched forward and fell face-first into his hat. His hat started to fill with blood. Fortunately, there was a bullet hole big enough to let the blood drain. Otherwise, he would have drowned in it.

GENERAL JOHN BROWN GORDON, C.S.A.

CAPTAIN TODD CARTER, C.S.A.

In 1861, Todd Carter, of Franklin, Tennessee, joined what would eventually become the Army of Tennessee. Four years later, he returned home when that Army's commander, John Bell Hood, launched a furious frontal assault on Federals holding Franklin on November 30, 1864. Some of the fiercest fighting took place right in front of the Carter's house. The Carters took refuge in their basement while fighting raged above them. Upon sighting his house, Todd cried out, "Follow me, boys, I'm almost home"! He was struck down near his house....and died two days later.

PRIVATE WESLEY CULP, C.S.A.

Gettysburg: during one of General Ewell's assaults on the right end of the Federal line on Culp's Hill, a young Private named Culp was killed. It was his own family farm on which he died. When the war broke out, Private Culp was attending school in South Carolina and, instead of returning home to fight for the Union, he joined the South Carolina militia, only to be present when the fighting at Gettysburg commenced. He was killed by Union fire while racing up the very same hill he'd played on as a child.

As General Lee walked into Mclean's house, he mistook Grant's aid as a Negro. When he realized that the man was an Indian, he shook the aid's hand and said, "I am glad to see one real American here." The man was Lt. Colonel Ely Parker, born "Hasanoanda", a sachem (or high chief) of the Seneca Nation. Parker gently replied to Lee, "We are all Americans, sir".

Some Mexican companies of the Confederate armies gained a reputation for unreliability. Private Juan Ivra was not of this stripe. In one Western action he staged a one-man charge into the faces of forty astonished Federals, and forced them to flee.

GENERAL J.E.B. STUART, C.S.A.

Confederate Lieutenant General. J.E.B. Stuart wore a beard because he had a "short and retiring" chin described by some as "girlish" which at West Point had earned him the nickname "Beauty".

Trying to stem the rout after the collapse of Confederate General John B. Hood's attack at Ezra Church, near Atlanta, on 28 July 1864, an officer shouted, "What are you running for?" One panicked soldier yelled back, "Bekase I kaint fly"! (sic)

It was said that on Stonewall Jackson's death, some angels came down to escort him into heaven, only to find that he had beaten them to it by making a rapid flank march. (Sworn to by a Confederate Veteran.)

Robert E. Lee died on October 12, 1870; just two days after a flood had swept the hill country. The Lexington undertaker was embarrassed to report that he had no coffins, since the three he had lately imported from Richmond had been swept away from his river wharf. Two young men volunteered to search for a coffin for the Lee funeral. They looked for hours before discovering one which had been swept over a dam and had lodged on an island some two miles downstream. Thus was provided the coffin in which the Confederacy's greatest figure was buried. The casket was too short for Lee and he was buried without his shoes.

Former U.S. President, John Tyler, was elected to the Confederate Senate as a Senator representing the Confederate State of Virginia.

Former U.S. Vice President and Presidential candidate, John Breckenridge, served the Confederacy as a Major General.

Abraham Lincoln's wife, Mary Todd Lincoln, had three relatives that served in the Confederate Army.

Patrick Henry's ("Give me Liberty or Give Me Death"!) Grandson fought at Gettysburg in the Confederate Army.

For some years before the War, Ambrose P. Hill courted a young beauty named Ellen Marcy. She jilted him and married his West Point roommate, George B. McClellan. Union troops attributed Hill's singular aggressiveness against his successful rival, so that during one attack, a Union veteran was heard to cry, "My God, Nellie, why didn't you marry him"?

The first income tax in American history was instituted by the Union on July 1, 1862; a measure which was copied in the Confederacy nine months later.

Francis Scott Key, the man who penned *"The Star Spangled Banner"*, would have been amazed that his entire family will later support the Southern Secession.

Miss Sally L. Tompkins, of Richmond, was made a Captain of Cavalry by Jefferson Davis on September 9, 1861. She became the only woman ever to hold a commission in the Confederate Army. Davis had been impressed that the hospital that she had created at the First Battle of Bull Run, (Manassas), had such a high recovery rate, and wanted to reward her.

Although bureaucracies are noted for such things as "procedural errors" and "administrative oversights", it is nevertheless still remarkable that the famed *U.S.S. MONITOR*, which went down in Force 7 winds off Cape Hatteras on December, 31 1862, was not officially declared "out of commission" by the U.S. Navy until nearly 91 years later, on September 30, 1951.

Among the many prisoners taken when Confederate Brigadier General Nathan Bedford Forrest's troopers captured Holly Springs, Mississippi, on 20 December, 1862, was Julia Grant, the wife of Union Major General Ulysses S. Grant. She was shortly passed through the lines.

Desperate for saltpeter necessary for the making of gunpowder, the Confederacy sent out agents around the South to collect deposits of it. John Harrelson, an agent in Selma, Alabama of the Confederate Nitre and Mining Bureau, advertised the following in the local paper: "The ladies of Selma are respectfully requested to preserve the chamber lye collected about their premises for the purpose of making nitre. A barrel will be sent around daily to collect it."

The troops of both sides very quickly learned that the barrel of a musket could hold nearly a pint of whiskey.

Allen Pinkerton, head of intelligence for the Army of the Potomac, is said to have evaluated the suitability of women to serve as agents by means of "Phrenology". Phrenology was an accepted 19th century science that promoted the idea that one's intelligence could be measured by the shape of the skull, and the locations of the bumps on the skull.

It is said that after a particularly wearing march shortly before the first battle of Bull Run, Stonewall Jackson posted only one sentry for his brigade, the "Gallant Jackson", himself.

When, during the Battle of Murfreesboro, Confederate Major General Benjamin Cheatham shouted "Forward, boys, and give 'em hell, boys!", his superior, Lieutenant General Leonidas Polk, agreeing in principal, but, as an Episcopal Bishop, unwilling to utter profanity, shouted "Give 'em what General Cheatham says, boys! Give 'em what General Cheatham says"!

As their gunboat was preparing to go into action, a Union naval officer asked a sailor why he was on his knees, to which the youthful tar replied, "Praying, sir, that the enemy's bullets may be distributed the same way as the prize money, principally among the officers".

When a Yankee sniper interrupted his service one Sunday morning, Confederate Chaplain Isaac T. Tichenor grabbed a musket, dispatched the man to his Maker, and went back to his prayers.

While on a riverine expedition in search of Rebels, Union Rear Admiral David Dixon Porter remarked, "Armies loot, Navies take prizes".

It required the personal intervention of Abraham Lincoln to get Congress to authorize the enlistment of chaplains of the Jewish Faith.

The youngest officer in the war was undoubtedly E.G. Baxter, (born 10 September 1849), who enlisted in the Confederate 7th Kentucky in June of 1862 and was made a second lieutenant when not quite 14.

When Corporal Mike Scannel, of the 19th Massachusetts, displayed some reluctance to carry the flag at Cold Harbor, his regimental commander said, "I'll make you a sergeant on the spot"! Scannel replied, "That's business...", grabbed the colors, and led the troops forward.

There were 39 Missouri regiments at the siege of Vicksburg, 22 in blue, and 17 in gray.

During the Battle of Kennesaw Mountain, (27 June 1864), a small woods, in which some Union wounded were sheltering, caught fire. Confederate Colonel W. H. Martin, of the 1st Arkansas, seeing the situation, jumped up on a parapet, waved a white flag, and shouted, "We won't fire until you get them away"! With that offer, a brief truce occurred while the Union wounded were evacuated. At the end of the battle, a Yankee major gave Martin a brace of pistols in gratitude for his brave and gallant gesture.

ILLUSTRATIONS BY THOMAS NAST

In the Thomas Nast cartoon that first depicted Santa Claus with a sleigh and reindeer, he was delivering Christmas gifts to Union soldiers. The cartoon entitled *"Santa Claus in Camp"*, appeared in *Harper's Weekly* on January 3, 1863.

(Point of trivia: The Great State of Alabama was the first State in the U.S. that made Christmas a Legal Holiday in 1836.)

"Hiding the Pickle" was a tradition during this time. A glass pickle was hidden on the tree by St. Nicholas on Christmas Eve. The child who found it on Christmas morning got a special gift from the old elf.

SGT. JOHN LINCOLN CLEM, U.S.A.

The last Civil War veteran on active duty was John Lincoln Clem, who had signed up as a drummer boy at 8 in 1861; he retired as a major general in 1916. He was credited with killing a Rebel officer during the Battle of Chickamauga at the age of 10.

U.S. Grant's memoirs, completed shortly before his death in 1885 was published by his friend Mark Twain; it earned $450,000 in royalties. (Close to $10.4 million in today's money.)

Not until World War II, did the United States Army realize it was no longer necessary for soldiers to have perfect teeth in order to bite their paper cartridges; a large number of men with malocclusions suddenly became I-A.

At the gate to the cemetery in Gettysburg, where some of the heaviest fighting took place on the first day of the battle, there was a sign which read, "All persons found using firearms in these grounds will be prosecuted with the utmost rigor of the law".

At one point in the war, the Yankee 7th Tennessee was captured by the Rebel 7th Tennessee.

U. S. Grant smoked about two dozen cigars a day.

Pierre G.T. Beauregard had the shortest tenure of any superintendent of West Point; it ran from 23 to 28 January, 1861. He was dismissed for seditious behavior.

So infrequently did Thomas "Stonewall" Jackson draw his sword, that it eventually rusted in the scabbard...so the tale is told.

While enduring the Confederate bombardment atop Cemetery Ridge on the third day of Gettysburg, Union General John Gibbon may perhaps have received some satisfaction from the knowledge that the enemy was using his own manual, *The Artillerist's Manual*, as their basic handbook.

When the Orleans Guards, a Louisiana volunteer battalion, went into action at Shiloh, they discovered that their stylish blue uniforms had the unfortunate effect of causing their Rebel comrades to mistake them for Yankees. They reversed their coats and fought all day with the white linings showing.

When Union troops captured Fort Pulaski, Georgia, on April 11, 1862, the newly appointed commander, Col. Alfred H. Terry of the 7th Connecticut, summoned his Confederate predecessor, a Colonel Olmstead, and lent him $50 to tide him over for any inconvenience which might occur while he was a prison-of-war.

George S. Lamkin, of Winona, Mississippi, joined Stanford's Mississippi Battery when he was eleven, and before his twelfth birthday, was severely wounded at Shiloh.

AND FINALLY..... When questioned by some Indiana troops as to whether she was "Secesh" or "Union", an old mountain woman replied, "A Baptist, an' always have been"!

Battles With Dual Names		
Date of Battle	**Confederate Name**	**Federal Name**
July 21, 1861	First Manassas	Bull Run
Aug. 10, 1861	Oak Hills	Wilson's Creek
Oct. 21, 1861	Leesburg	Ball's Bluff
Jan. 19, 1862	Mill Springs	Logan's Cross Roads
Mar. 7-8, 1862	Elkhorn Tavern	Pea Ridge
Apr. 6-7, 1862	Shiloh	Pittsburg Landing
June 27, 1862	Gaines's Mill	Chickahominy
Aug. 29-30,1862	Second Manassas	Second Bull Run
Sept. 1, 1862	Ox Hill	Chantilly
Sept. 14, 1862	Boonsboro	South Mountain

Sept. 17, 1862	Sharpsburg	Antietam
Oct. 8, 1862	Perryville	Chaplin Hills
Dec. 31, 1862- Jan. 2, 1863	Murfreesboro	Stones River
Apr. 8, 1864	Mansfield	Sabine Cross Roads
Sept. 19, 1864	Winchester	Opequon Creek

Even though women weren't legally allowed to join the military during the Civil War, it is estimated that somewhere around 400 women disguised themselves as men and went to war, sometimes without anyone ever discovering their true identities. At least one woman served as a "drummer boy" during the war. A Brooklyn resident named "Emily" disguised herself as a boy and enlisted in Michigan. While serving, she was mortally wounded at Lookout Mountain, near Chattanooga.

During the War, a woman was brought into General J.E.B. Stuart's command tent. She was being exposed as an imposter, and was dressed as a man. General Stuart eyed the woman briefly, and, according to reports, told her bluntly that she was going to prison in Richmond.

The woman feigned a couple of tears and exclaimed, "But, General, I'm a WOMAN"!

Stuart raised his eyes once again from his papers and said, "Madam, you joined this army as a man, you can go to prison as one". She was placed on a horse and led away.

DR. MARY WALKER

AMERICA'S ONLY FEMALE MEDAL OF HONOR WINNER

Born the youngest of five daughters in Oswego, New York, Mary Walker worked hard on their family farm while being tutored by her mother in a local school. Mary refused to wear women's clothing to do the farm chores, as she found them too restricting. As a young woman, she later taught at the same school to earn enough money to pay her way through Syracuse Medical College, (now Upstate Medical University). She graduated as a medical doctor in 1855, and was the only woman in her class. She married a fellow medical school student, Albert, and they set up a joint practice in Rome, New York.

Their practice did not fare well because of the stigma still attached to women in the Arts. After attending another University, (and being kicked out of school for not giving up her spot on the "all-male" debating team), she eventually volunteered for the United State Army as a civilian when the War broke out.

At first, she was only allowed to practice as a nurse, as the U.S. Army had no female surgeons. During this period, she served at the First Battle of Bull Run, (Manassas), July 21, 1861, and at the Patent Office Hospital in Washington, D.C.. She later worked as an unpaid field surgeon near the Union front lines, including the

Battle of Fredericksburg and in Chattanooga after the Battle of Chickamauga.

In September of 1862, Walker wrote to the War Department requesting employment in the Secret Service to spy for the Union. The offer was sternly declined. Finally, she was employed as a "Contract Acting Assistant Surgeon", (civilian), by the Army of the Cumberland in September of 1863. She became the first-ever female surgeon employed by the U.S. Army.

Walker was later appointed assistant surgeon of the 52nd Ohio Infantry. During this service, she frequently crossed battle lines to treat civilians. On April 10, 1864, she was captured by Confederate troops and arrested as a spy, just after she finished helping a Confederate doctor perform an amputation. She was sent to Richmond, Virginia and remained there until August 12, 1864 when she was released as part of a prisoner exchange. She went on to serve during the Battle of Atlanta, and later as supervisor of a female prison in Louisville, Kentucky. She also ran an orphanage in Tennessee toward the end of her incredible career.

MARY: CIRCA 1867   MARY: CIRCA 1911

When the War ended, Walker was recommended for the Medal of Honor by Generals William Tecumseh Sherman and George

Henry Thomas. On November 11, 1865, President Andrew Johnson signed a bill to award her the medal.

The U.S. Congress created a pension act for Medal of Honor recipients in 1917, and, in doing so, created separate Army and Navy Medal of Honor Rolls. The Army, alone, decided to review eligibility for inclusion on the Army Medal of Honor Roll. The 1917 Medal of Honor Board never rescinded any medals in 1917 but, instead, deleted 911 names from the Army Medal of Honor Roll. Two of those names rescinded were Dr. Mary Edwards Walker and William F. "Buffalo Bill" Cody. None of the 911 recipients were ordered to return their medals, but there was a debate as to whether those recipients could continue to wear their medals. The Judge Advocate General advised the Medal of Honor Board that there was no obligation on the Army to police the matter. Walker continued to wear her medal until her death.

Mary Walker lectured frequently for the Women's Suffragette Movement, and was known to dress like a man most of the time, including the top hat and frock coat.

President Jimmy Carter restored her medal, posthumously, in 1977.

INVENTIONS OF OUR TIME

As amazing as it may seem to some, we were a lot further advanced in our inventions and technology in 1860 than most people have remembered. I have assembled a list of some of those inventions along with their dates... just for fun.

1760....Roller skates were invented.

1760....Jigsaw puzzles were introduced by John Spilsbury.

1765....Pencils were commercially produced in Germany.

1767....Joseph Priestly produced the first "soft drink" by introducing carbonated water. (It tasted terrible, and no one would drink it.)

1780....Baker's chocolate was introduced by John Hannan.

1780....William Addis designed the first modern toothbrush having a handle and bristles. The handle was wooden; the bristles were made from boar's hair.

1793....Cotton gin was designed by Eli Whitney and Catherine Greene. (Catherine was the widow of General Nathaniel Greene.)

1793....First sewing thread was introduced by Hannah Slater.

1796....Edward Jenner prepared the first effective vaccine for smallpox.

1799....Powdered chlorine bleach was introduced in England by Charles Tennant.

1799....Dr. Hinkling was the first to apply enamel to saucepans.

1803....Carbon paper was invented by Ralph Wedgewood.

1803....Steel pen nibs were patented.

1806....Soap was manufactured by William Colgate.

1806....Nicholas Appert developed a process for preserving food, (for the French Military), in glass containers, (sealed by cork), by means of a hot water bath.

1807....Townsend Speakman mixed fruit flavors with Priestley's carbonated water and marketed the first soda pop called "Nephite Julip".

1809....Humphry Davy invents the first electric light; the first arc lamp.

1810....An Englishman named Peter Durand preserved foods in tin and iron cans, as well as pottery and glass containers, by means of a hot water bath, heat, and steam bath; the container was sealed later.

1814....Joseph Nicéphore Niépce was the first known person to take a photograph. He took the picture by setting up a machine called the "camera obscura" in the window of his home in France. It took eight hours for the camera to take the picture.

FIRST PERMANENT PHOTO EVER TAKEN (Roof top in Paris.)

1815....The James Cook Stove was patented in Troy, New York.

1816....Pedestrian Hobby Horse, (crude bicycle), was invented by Karl von Drais. It was foot-powered with no pedals.

1816....Monaural stethoscope was designed by Frenchman L. Laennec.

1819....Chocolate, in bar form, was introduced by Francois Cailler, (Switzerland).

1819....Ezra Daggett and Thomas Kensett introduced canned salmon, oysters and lobsters in New York City.

1821....The Harmonica was invented by Christian Friedric Buschmann.

1822.....Quinine was manufactured in Philadelphia, Pennsylvania.

1822....William Underwood Company introduced "tinned meat", (Underwood Deviled Ham).

1824....Portland Cement, an artificial stone, was quarried on the Ile of Portland, (in the English Channel), developed by Joseph Aspdin.

1824....Michael Faraday invented the first toy balloon.

1824....William Sturgeon invented the electromagnet.

1825....Plans for a home refrigerator, (the ice box), were published.

1827....Charles Wheatstone was the first person to coin the

phrase "microphone." (A microphone is a device for converting acoustic power into electric power that has essentially similar wave characteristics. Microphones convert sound waves into electrical voltages that are eventually converted back into sound waves thru speakers. They were first used with early telephones and then radio transmitters.)

1827....Concentrated milk, (evaporated milk), was developed.

1828....Cocoa powder was patented by C. J. van Houton.

1828....Henry Leroux found a pain relieving substance in willow, (salacin), but it was not developed.

1829....American, W. A. Burt, invents a typewriter.

1829....Frenchmen, Louis Braille, invents "Braille", printing for the blind.

1829....William Austin Burt patents a "typographer", a predecessor to the modern typewriter.

1829....Sylvester Graham introduced the Graham Cracker as a breakfast cereal.

1829....Sewing machine invented by Bartholemy Themonnier, (improved model in 1848).

1830....Reel lawnmower was invented.

1830....Cakes of soap of uniform weight were individually wrapped by Jessie Oakley.

1830....Steel pen nibs produced by machine.

1832....Bedsprings were patented by Josiah French.

1831....Elastic webbing, (rubber wrapped in thread), was patented in Britain.

1831....Chloroform was used by Samuel Guthrie.

1832....Machine for manufacturing pins was patented by J. I. Howe.

1832....Long stitch sewing machine invented by Walter Hunt.

1832....John Matthews invents the first soda fountain which made and dispensed soda water.

1834....Sandpaper was patented by Isaac Fisher.

1834....Valentine cards were first commercially printed.

1834....Reaper was patented by Cyrus McCormick.

1834....The phosphorous friction match was patented by A.D. Phillips.

1834....Wire sieve was manufactured commercially.

1834....Jacob Perkins patented the first mechanical refrigerator.

1834....."Baseball" was included in *The Book of Sports*.

1835....Charles Babbage invents a mechanical calculator.

1835....Telegraph was invented by Samuel Morse.

1836....Revolver was invented by Samuel Colt.

1836....Hook and eye fasteners were manufactured.

1837....Underwater diving suit was used by Augustus Siebe.

1837....Stenographic shorthand was developed by Isaac Pitman.

1837....John Deere developed a modern plow that would break up the western plains.

1839....Vulcanized rubber was invented by accident by Charles Goodyear.

1839....Frenchmen, Louis Daguerre and Joseph Nicéphore Niépce, co-invent Daguerreotype photography.

NIEPCE   **DAGUERRE**

1839....Flexible stethoscope was made by C.W. Pennock.

1839....Clarke produced enameled kitchenware items such as preserving kettles, soup and stew pots.

1840....Electric clock was invented by Alexander Bain. Electric current was generated from coke and zinc plates buried in the ground.

1840s....Commercial starch was introduced by Reckitt and Sons.

1841....Elastic webbing was patented by Henry Hubbard in Middletown, Connecticut.

1842....Postage stamps with adhesive were introduced in New York City.

1842....Cornstarch was patented by Thomas Kingsford.

1842....Ether was used by Dr. Crawford Long in Georgia, but he did not publish the results until 1849.

1843....Christmas cards were introduced in England by Henry Cole.

1843....Alexander Bain, of Scotland, invents the facsimile.

1844....Nitrous oxide was introduced by Dr. Horace Wells.

1844....Morse's first electronic telegram was sent and received.

1844....Ice making machine was patented by Dr. John Gurrie, (used as an air conditioner for fevered patients).

1845....Dr. Horace Day and Dr. William Shecutt patented the "Band Aid", an adhesive plaster painted with rubber dissolved in a solvent; known as "Allcocks Pourous Plaster".

1845....Sulfuric acid was made by John Robuck.

1845....Rubber band was patented by Stephen Perry.

1845....Gelatin dessert was patented by Peter Cooper, (improved by Pearl and May Wit, and sold for $450.00; It was renamed "Jell-O" in 1895.)

1845....Sewing machine was patented by Elias Howe that lock-stitched and sewed 250 stitches a minute.

1845....Soap packets were sold in individual packets by B. T. Babbitt.

1845....Crawford Long used ether on a woman in childbirth.

1846....Baking saleratus, (baking soda), introduced by John Dwight and Austin Church.

1846....Crinoline, (made of woven horsehair), was introduced.

1846....Dr. William Morton, a Massachusetts dentist, is the first to use anesthesia for tooth extraction.

1846....Ether was used in Massachusetts by Dr. John Warren.

1846....Nitroglycerine was invented.

1846....Kerosene wax, (from coal oil or shale oil), was used to fuel lamps.

1846....Ice Cream maker was invented by Nancy Johnson, but not patented.

1847....Cough drops were introduced by the Smith Brothers.

1847....Hungarian Ignaz Semmelweis invents antiseptics.

1847....Oliver Chase invented a candy machine to cut candy lozenges known as "Peerless Waffers" (sic), (now known as NECCO Wafers).

1847....Sylvester Graham introduces bread made with whole wheat, unbolted flour (unsifted).

1848....Ice cream maker was patented by William Young.

1848....Salt company organized in Chicago, (to become Morton Salt Company in 1895).

1848....Baby carriage was introduced by Charles Burton.

1848....Macaroni factory was built in Brooklyn.

1848....The first department store, Marble Dry Goods Palace, was opened in New York City by Alexander Stewart.

1849....Dr. Elizabeth Blackwell was the first woman physician graduated from Geneva Medical College.

1849....Walter Hunt invents the safety pin.

1850....Women's Medical College of Pennsylvania was the first regular medical college opened for women.

1850....Isaac Singer invents his sewing machine.

1852....Steel ribbed umbrellas introduced in England.

1853....The Potato Chip was invented by George Crum. Crum was a Native- American/African-American chef at the Moon Lake Lodge resort in Saratoga Springs, New York. French, (home), fries were popular at the restaurant and, one day, a diner complained that the fries were too thick. Although Crum made a thinner batch, the customer was still unsatisfied. Crum finally made fries that were too thin to eat with a fork, hoping to annoy the extremely fussy customer. The customer, surprisingly enough, was happy - and potato chips were invented! These chips were originally called "Saratoga Chips".

1853....George Cayley invents a manned-glider.

1854....John Tyndall demonstrates the principles of fiber optics.

1854....Breast pump patented by O.H. Needham.

1856....Louis Pasteur invents pasteurization.

1856....Isaac Singer markets his sewing machine by introducing the Nation's first "Installment Program". The purchase of a sewing machine involved $5.00 down and $3.00 a month. (The average family income in 1856 was $500.00 a year.) By 1860, 100,000 machines had been sold.

1856....Bessemer converter used to make steel.

1856....Condensed milk was introduced by Gail Borden.

1856....Shoe manufacturing machine was developed.

1856....Hoops made with bone or steel, replaces the need for bulky crinoline.

1857....Toilet paper in individual sheets was introduced by Joseph Gayetty, called "Gayetty's Medicated Paper".

1857....Harmonica was marketed by Matthias Hohner.

1857....George Pullman invents the Pullman Sleeping Car for train travel.

1857... Pink lemonade first offered.

1858....Jean Lenoir invents an internal combustion engine.

1858....Hand-held can-opener introduced.

1858....Jars with screw-on lids were patented by John Landis Mason. (Attempted a salt shaker in 1859... did not catch on.)

1858....Pencil with built-in eraser was patented by Hyman Lipman.

1858....Ironing board introduced.

1859....Fluorescent bulb was invented by Alexandre Edmond Becquerel, (80 years before it was perfected).

1859....Hand-powered vacuum cleaner was introduced.

1860s... Hot dogs were introduced in New York City; bun replaced plate for convenience.

1860....Manufactured cigarettes make their debut.

1861....Elisha Otis patents elevator safety brakes, creating a safer elevator.

1861.....Pierre Michaux invents a pedal-version of the bicycle.

1861.....Linus Yale invents the Yale lock or cylinder lock.

1861.....Jelly beans are introduced.

1862.....Richard Gatling patents the machine gun.

1862.....The first federal tax on cigarettes was levied to pay for the Civil War.

1862.....Alexander Parkes invents the first man-made plastic.

1863.....Modern, steerable roller skates invented by James Plimpton.

1863.....Breakfast cereal introduced, "Granula" (sic). Had to soak all night to soften it up. Later became "Grape-Nuts".

1864... First submarine to sink a ship in combat: *THE H. L. HUNLEY*, (Confederate), attacked and sank a Union ship, *THE U.S.S. HOUSATONIC*, on February 17, 1864.

H. L. HUNLEY, CONFEDERATE SUBMARINE

A CONFEDERATE INVENTION

LT. COLONEL JOHN STITH PEMBERTON, C.S.A.

INVENTOR OF COCA-COLA

Confederate and combat veteran John Pemberton (1830-1888), invented Coca-Cola on May 8th, 1886 in Atlanta, Georgia. He had invented many syrups, medicines, and elixirs, including a very popular drink called *French Wine of Coca*, which contained French Bordeux wine, cocaine, and caffeine, (from the kola nut). When Atlanta banned alcohol consumption in 1885, Pemberton had to change the formula of his *French Wine of Coca*, omitting the French wine.

He added sugar, citric acid and essential oils of many fruits to the drink, and the original Coca-Cola was created, (named for its main ingredients, cocaine and the kola nut). It quickly became a very popular soda fountain drink.

Pemberton became partners with Frank Robinson and David Roe, but the partnership soon quarreled. Pemberton sold his interest in Coca-Cola. Cocaine is no longer an ingredient of Coca-Cola, but caffeine, sugar, citric acid, and fruit oils remain, (although the formula is a closely-guarded secret). Just wanted to let you know that when you take a sip of Coke, think about the South.

CHAPTER TWELVE

THE TRUTH ABOUT THE SONG *DIXIE*

In 1859, the song that would come to be known as *"Dixie"* debuted in a New York theater. It was written by a Northerner named Daniel Decatur Emmett of Mt. Vernon, Ohio. *Dixie* was written as a minstrel song for live theater. It tells a story of a slave's "ol missus" and her husband "Will de weaber". There are conflicting stories of its origins, and, as best I can figure, this is the story:

Daniel Decatur Emmett was friends with the Snowdens, an African-American family of slave origin. They lived close by Emmett's home in or around Mt. Vernon, Ohio.

The Snowdens were a talented musical family that performed regularly in a 75 mile radius of their home. They may have influenced him in this song, it is hard to tell. Time lines are conflicting, and the sources are dubious and tainted with local legends and wishful thinking. A photo of Daniel Emmet was found in the personal effects of the Snowdens after their deaths, along with newspaper clippings about him. (We are still looking for the missing link.)

As the War seemed certain, this little "ditty" became more at the center of public focus. Its message and meaning became more politically poignant and became a regional "battle cry". The words *"In Dixie Land, I'll take my stand, to live and die in Dixie"!* rang true to the Southern heart. When the troops began to march north, this became their anthem and call for secession.

The Civil War ended in 1865, yet *"Dixie"* remained a regional anthem in the South. With time, National politics and forced-integration created a split in the interpretation of the song. People sing it or hate it for their own reasons.

I believe that it became a political football during the early Civil

Rights Era. It was the focus of African-American leaders who could not deal with their own issues and could not answer the real problems within their communities. Like politicians of all stripes, they took the easy road, got face-time on TV, and secured themselves a leadership role without solving much of anything. These are my opinions, of course; some will disagree. It is so easy to attack targets like the *Confederate Battle Flag* and *Dixie*.

THE DIXIECRATS AND THE FLAGS

What the Press did not tell you was that this symbol of the old Confederacy became a symbol of hate in contemporary times when it was selected by part of the Democrat Party in 1948.

After Truman became President, he regarded the treatment of our Black Veterans by America as abhorrent, and he decided he would take the lead to do something about it.

By an Executive Order in 1948, Truman began the integration of the United States Military, starting with the Army in 1948. Southern Democrats bolted as more Northern Democrats were suggesting that we integrate the entire Nation. The early days for "Equal Rights" were causing a split the Nation.

The Southern Democrats broke away and re-named their Party "The States Rights Democratic Party"; they were nicknamed "The Dixiecrats". They met in Convention in Birmingham, Alabama on July 17, 1948, and chose Senator Strom Thurmond from South Carolina to be their candidate; Governor Fielding L. Wright from Mississippi to run as Vice President. They won four states in 1948.

The roots of the Dixiecrat revolt lay in opposition to the New Deal policies, particularly the pro-labor reforms introduced by the Fair Labor Standards Act and the Wagner Act. The more immediate impetus for the movement, however, included President Harry Truman's civil rights program, introduced in February 1948; the civil rights plank in the national Democratic Party's 1948 presidential platform; and the unprecedented political mobilization of Southern Blacks in the wake of the U.S. Supreme Court decision in *Smith v. Allwright* in 1944.

In this Texas case, the Court ruled the White Primary Law violated the Fifteenth Amendment and was therefore unconstitutional. The states of the Upper South acquiesced in the ruling, but the decision was a political bombshell in the Deep South. White legislators, across the region, sought ways to circumvent the ruling, and African-Americans organized voter-registration campaigns. Across the South, more than a half million African-Americans registered to vote in the 1946 Democratic Party primaries.

It was at this "Dixiecrat" convention in Birmingham that the delegates chose the Confederate Battle Flag as their Party's new standard; all these years later, look at the results. The "hate" began in 1948, brought to you by Southern Democrats.

The very Party that embraces the African-American Vote today was the Party that strove for their exclusion in 1948. Time passed, things changed, and minority votes became critical; guess who loves the African-American community now? Politics make strange bedfellows, indeed.

I need not tell you how much damage the Democrats did to the Old South when they made that decision in 1948; you know, yourself, how it turned out. But, why didn't you know this?

The reason that the general public has little or no knowledge of this is simple: our modern Press is Pro-Democrat, and our school system is part of the same political clime. This info was simply left out of your school books along with the fact that the *Battle Flag* was not raised above the South Carolina Capitol until 1962 by former Dixiecrats; leave a little out and change the story.

It was raised by the same group of racists, The Dixiecrats, with the leadership of Democrat Fritz Hollings, and the Democrat-controlled South Carolina Legislature.

I find it ironic that the very politicians who want the symbol down are of the same group who put it up... and who blamed the Republicans for the whole event. The Press knows better......

Study photos of the Klan rallies before 1948... you will see NO *Confederate Battle Flags* in any photo made before that Birmingham Convention. Hollywood inserts these flags in movies during times when they were not used, and these images are adding to the divide that continues to grow between the races in America. The Press and Hollywood make millions of dollars stirring up the pot. They are merchants in chaos and hate.

I lived through those times as many of you did; I speak from my own view point, of course. Our young people have no real clue.

One can access almost every newspaper ever printed in this Nation and read the very words spoken at the time by all of our Politicians. Read the front pages of the South Carolina papers during 1961 and 1962. Read the words spoken by those Democrat leaders. It will amaze you, and make you think: what else have we not been told?

Today's Press has quicker access to all of this than I do. They could have told you; they chose not to. Now you know why.

TO SUMMARIZE

Dixie and the *Confederate Battle Flag* are complicated issues. It is true that Confederates sang *Dixie* as they marched off to war, but an anti-slavery Northerner, Daniel Emmett, wrote it. It may have been played at the inauguration of Confederate President Jefferson Davis, but Abraham Lincoln had it played at his Ball, as well. The song's humor may rest on a parody of Black speech and behavior, but it is a fact that Dan Emmett actually learned the language from current speech and possibly from an affiliation to the Snowden family, the Black minstrel theater group from Knox County, Ohio. *The Battle Flag* also had numerous duties for numerous groups at different times.

Taking a song written in 1858 and critiquing it with 21st Century views is a fool's game, played by fools who want nothing but division in this country. I might point out that a lot of Free Blacks fought for that song and flag, as well.

These are two of the many photos of Black Confederate Veterans that you will not see in your local school books.

The 1830 U.S. Census listed 3,777 free Black slave owners holding a total of 12,740 slaves. Where are they in your school books?

Hiding African-American involvement in the Confederacy and slavery is racist to the core. Liberals deny Black students their heritage and then demand inclusion in the same breath. It is time to put all Americans back into our historical libraries; ALL OF THEM. Those who hide their history will lose it eventually.

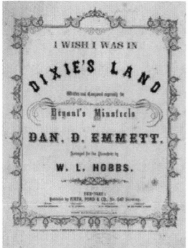

DIXIE'S LAND

By Daniel Decatur Emmett of Mount Vernon, Ohio

ORIGINAL SPELLING OF WORDS

Oh, I wish I was in de lan' ob cotton,
Old times dar am not forgotten.

(*Alt Original:* 'Simmon seeds and sandy bottom,)
Look away, look away, look away Dixie Land.

In Dixie Land, where I was born in,
early on one frosty mornin'.
Look away, look away, look away Dixie Land.

Den I wish I was in Dixie, Hooray! Hooray!
In Dixie Land I'll take my stand
to lib and die in Dixie.
Away, away, away down south in Dixie.
Away, away, away down south in Dixie.

Optional Verses

Ole Missus marry "Will the weaver."
Willum was a gay deceiver.
Look away! Look away! Look away!
Dixie Land.

But when he put his arm around 'er,
He smiled fierce as a forty pounder.
Look away! Look away! Look away!
Dixie Land.

His face was sharp as a butcher's cleaver,
But that did not seem to grieve 'er.
Look away! Look away! Look away!
Dixie Land.

229

Ole Missus acted the foolish part,
And died for a man that broke her heart.
Look away! Look away! Look away!
Dixie Land.

Now here's a health to the next ole Missus,
An' all the gals that want to kiss us.
Look away! Look away! Look away!
Dixie Land.

But if you want to drive 'way sorrow,
Come and hear this song tomorrow.
Look away! Look away! Look away!
Dixie Land.

There's buckwheat cakes and Injun batter,
Makes you fat or a little fatter.
Look away! Look away! Look away!
Dixie Land.

Then hoe it down and scratch your gravel,
To Dixie's Land I'm bound to travel.
Look away! Look away! Look away!
Dixie Land.

Emmett wrote in the vernacular of the time and I have left the words in this book in their original incarnation.

Emmett parodied the speech of most slaves of this time in the same way that Samuel Clements, (Mark Twain), will later in that century. If we leave the language alone, we will preserve an intangible nuance to a time that cannot be recovered once erased. Language has to be preserved in its virgin form.

Censorship is arrogance; arrogance becomes tyranny, and I do not use that word lightly, folks.

(Point of trivia: Some contemporary African-Americans use the term "axe" instead "ask". This was a word learned by their ancestors who were first brought here and were exposed to Old Elizabethan English. The term "axe" is a proper term for "to ask". During the 16th, 17th and 18th Centuries, "axe" was used by everyone who spoke English. An example, taken from The King James Version of the Bible: "...and Pilate 'axid' him (Jesus)." "Axid" is the proper spelling and pronunciation of the past tense of "axe". The first book of etiquette in the United States was published in 1862, and has that word listed in the Index as a word that was considered "obsolete, and shouldn't be used anymore." Some folks got the e-mail, some folks didn't. Point two: The word "aint" means to "have not". It evolved from "haint". "Haint" was used more in personal letters of our troops in the 19th century and was a left-over from the same source as the older Elizabethan English. The words "reckon" and "yonder" are considered "red-neck" when they are actually Old English. Re-read some Shakespeare; that ole' boy "reckoned" and "yondered" all over England. As far as I know, William Shakespeare never drove a pick-up truck with a number "3" on the side.)

It is important, again, to note that when one messes with the original spelling, they are altering history. The use of this symbol "(sic)" is used to explain that the word is left in its original state and was not a type-o. I used it a lot.

So, regardless of the effect this will have on my readers, it is the only way to re-emphasize the idea that we are NOT our relatives, and we cannot judge history, we can analyze it.

"It is a fool who will judge history; and a wise man who will learn from it."

....."GRANDDADDY'S WATCH" by Steve Gipson

CAN A STATE LEGALLY SECEDE?

Four bloody years of war ended what had been the most significant attempt by states to secede from the Union. While the South was forced to abandon its dreams of a new Southern Confederacy, many of its people have never accepted the idea that secession was a violation of the U.S. Constitution, basing their arguments primarily on Article X of that Constitution:

"The powers not delegated to the United States by the Constitution, nor prohibited by it to the States, are reserved to the States respectively, or to the people."

The on-going debate continues over the question that has been asked since the forming of the United States itself: "Can a state secede from the Union of the United States"? Whether it is legal for a state to secede from the United States is a question that was fiercely debated before the Civil War and, even now, that debate continues. From time to time, new calls have arisen for one state or another to secede, in reaction to political and/or social changes. Organizations, such as the League of the South, openly support secession and the formation of a new Southern Republic.

Southerners insisted they could legally bolt from the Union; Northerners swore they could not. War would settle the matter...but for how long? Time will tell.

Over the centuries, various excuses have been employed for starting wars. Wars have been fought over land, honor, religion and sectional disputes, among others.

The Civil War was largely fought over equally compelling interpretations of the U.S. Constitution. Which side was the Constitution on? That's difficult to say. The interpretative debate—and ultimately the War—turned on the intent of the framers of the Constitution and the meaning of a single word:

"sovereignty"—which does not actually appear anywhere in the text of the Constitution, ironically enough.

Southern leaders, like John C. Calhoun and Jefferson Davis, argued that the Constitution was essentially a contract between "sovereign states"—with the contracting parties retaining the inherent authority to withdraw from the agreement. Northern leaders, like Abraham Lincoln, insisted the Constitution was neither a contract nor an agreement between "sovereign states". It was an agreement with the "people", and once a state enters the Union, it cannot leave the Union. I have to wonder where he got that idea. How is that logical? You can join and can't quit? There is absolutely nothing in the Constitution that says that a State cannot leave. Where is the true concept of freedom?

A SERIOUS LOOK AT THE DEBATE

It is a touchstone of American constitutional law that this is a nation based on federalism—the union of states, which retain all rights not expressly given to the federal government. After the Declaration of Independence, when most people still identified themselves not as Americans but as Virginians, New Yorkers or Rhode Islanders, this union of "Free and Independent States" was defined as a "confederation". Some framers of the Constitution, like Maryland's Luther Martin, argued the new states were "separate sovereignties". Others, like Pennsylvania's James Wilson, took the opposite view that the states "were independent, not 'Individually' but 'unitedly'". (sic)

Supporting the individual sovereignty claims is the fierce independence that was asserted by states under the Articles of Confederation and Perpetual Union, which actually established the name "The United States of America". The charter, however, was careful to maintain the inherent sovereignty of its composite state elements, mandating that "each state retains its sovereignty, freedom, and independence, and every power, jurisdiction, and right, which is not by this Confederation

233

expressly delegated". It affirmed the sovereignty of the respective states by declaring, "The said states hereby severally enter into a firm league of friendship with each other for their common defense". There would seem little question that the states agreed to the Confederation on the express recognition of their sovereignty and relative independence.

Supporting the later view of Lincoln, the "perpetuality" (sic) of the Union was referenced during the Confederation period. For example, the Northwest Ordinance of 1787 stated that "the said territory, and the States which may be formed therein, shall forever remain a part of this confederacy of the United States of America".

The Confederation produced endless conflicts as various states issued their own money, resisted national obligations, and favored their own citizens in disputes. President James Madison criticized the Articles of Confederation as reinforcing the view of the Union as "a league of sovereign powers, not as a political Constitution by virtue of which they are become one sovereign power". Madison warned that such a view could lead to the "dissolving of the United States altogether". If the matter had ended there with the Articles of Confederation, Lincoln would have had a much weaker case for the court of law in taking up arms to preserve the Union. His legal case was saved by an 18th-century " bait and switch", the Constitutional Convention.

The Convention was called in 1787 to *amend* the Articles of Confederation, but several delegates eventually concluded that a new political structure—a federation—was needed. As they debated what would become the Constitution, the status of the states was a primary concern. George Washington, who presided over the convention, noted, "It is obviously impracticable in the federal government of these states, to secure all rights of independent sovereignty to each, and yet provide for the interest and safety of all". Of course, Washington was more concerned with a working federal government—and national army—than resolving the question of a state's inherent right to withdraw from such a union. The new government forged in Philadelphia would have clear lines of authority for the federal system. The premise of the Constitution, however, was that states would still hold all rights not expressly given to the federal government.

The final version of the Constitution never actually refers to the states as "sovereign", which, for many at the time, was the ultimate legal game-changer. In the U.S. Supreme Court's landmark 1819 decision in McCulloch v. Maryland, Chief Justice John Marshall espoused the view later embraced by Lincoln: "The government of the Union...is emphatically and truly, a government of the people". One man on the Supreme Court changed all of this? Some, at the time, resolved to leave the matter unresolved—and thereby planted the seed that would grow into a full civil war; did Lincoln win by force of arms or force of argument? That is the question, isn't it?

On January 21, 1861, Jefferson Davis went to the well of the U.S. Senate one last time to announce that he had "satisfactory evidence that the State of Mississippi, by a solemn ordinance of her people in convention assembled, has declared her separation from the United States". Before resigning his Senate seat, Davis laid out the basis for Mississippi's legal claim, coming down squarely on the fact that in the Declaration of Independence "the communities were declaring their independence"—not "the people". He added, "I have for many years advocated, as an essential attribute of state sovereignty, the right of a state to secede from the Union".

Davis' position reaffirmed that of John C. Calhoun. He had long viewed the states as independent sovereign entities. In an 1833 speech upholding the right of his home state to nullify federal tariffs it believed were unfair, Calhoun insisted, "I go on the ground that [the] constitution was made by the States; that it is a federal union of the States, in which the several States still retain their sovereignty". Calhoun allowed that a state could be barred from secession by a vote of two-thirds of the states under Article

V, which lays out the procedure for amending the Constitution.

Lincoln's Inauguration, on March 4, 1861, was used as a rallying cry for secession, and he became the head of a country that was falling apart, even as he raised his hand to take the oath of office. His first inaugural address left no doubt about his legal position: "No State, upon its own mere motion, can lawfully get out of the Union, that resolves and ordinances to that effect are legally void, and that acts of violence, within any State or States, against the authority of the United States, are insurrectionary or revolutionary, according to circumstances".

While Lincoln expressly called for a peaceful resolution, this was the final straw for many in the South who saw the speech as a not so veiled threat. Clearly, when Lincoln took the oath to "preserve, protect, and defend" the Constitution, he considered himself bound to preserve the Union as the physical creation of the Declaration of Independence and a central subject of the Constitution. This was made plain in his next major legal argument—an address where Lincoln rejected the notion of sovereignty for states as an "ingenious sophism" that would lead "to the complete destruction of the Union".

In a Fourth of July message to a special session of Congress in 1861, Lincoln declared, "Our States have neither more, nor less power, than that reserved to them, in the Union, by the Constitution—no one of them ever having been a State out of the Union. The original ones passed into the Union even before they cast off their British colonial dependence; and the new ones each came into the Union directly from a condition of dependence, excepting Texas. And even Texas, in its temporary independence, was never designated a State". Really? These colonies were *sovereign* entities when they cast out those English governors.

It is a flawed framing of the issue, which Lincoln proceeds to characterize as nothing less than an attack on the very notion of democracy: but he did note one telling difference: "Our adversaries have adopted some Declarations of Independence; in which, unlike the good old one, penned by Jefferson, they omit the words 'all men are created equal'". Lincoln was a hypocrite.

Our popular government has often been called an experiment. Two points in it our people have already settled—the successful establishing, and the successful administering of it. One still remains—its successful maintenance. That one is still in the air.

Moreover, while neither the Declaration of Independence nor the Constitution says states cannot secede, they also do not guarantee states such a right nor refer to the states as sovereign entities. While Calhoun's argument that Article V allows for changing the Constitution is attractive on some levels, Article V is designed to amend the Constitution, not the Union, per se. A clearly better argument could be made for a duly enacted amendment to the Constitution that would allow secession. In such a case, Lincoln would clearly have been warring against the democratic process he claimed to defend.

The North, in my view, maintained a self-serving argument. The ambiguous language in the Constitutional documents, however, muddies the view about the original states retaining the sovereign authority to secede from the Union. Greater minds than mine will have to keep pondering this one. I will add that with our current Supreme Court, I believe that our Constitution died recently with the Obama Care decision, and that any argument with real Constitutional depth is impossible. Lincoln would probably win this argument today in Robert's Court: "Politically-Correct" trumps the Law. That's the true danger.

Needless to say, Jefferson Davis was inherently vague when he provoked his fellow Mississippians with this statement, "Will you be slaves or will you be independent? Will you consent to be robbed of your property [or] strike bravely for liberty, property, honor and life"? Non-slaveholders—the majority of Southerners—were bombarded with similarly inflammatory rhetoric designed to paint Northerners as integrationist aggressors scheming to make blacks the equal of whites and impose race-mixing on a helpless population. The propaganda was thick on *both* sides, not to mention, effective.

One has to ask himself if there was anything that could have stopped this War from happening? I really don't think so.

EPILOGUE

I would like to sum this book up with some last minute thoughts and observations. During this process, I have uncovered more areas that I will write about in my next effort. Here are some final words for now.

This gradual elimination of inclusive facts only dilute history, distort it for our youth, and cause confusion in the minds of the common citizen who simply believes what they see published by our press, our schools, and our government.

The lack of a Confederate historical presence in a lot of State web-sites and printed material indicates the subtle censorship and the pandering to special groups by State and national government officials. They do this blindly at the cost of weakening us as a people. Division created by this form of censorship is going to prove fatal to us as a Nation if the tide isn't turned. Government should show no bias in these matters.

(Point of trivia: All of the literature, issued by the State of Virginia, available at the Visitor's Centers, depict only Black Union re-enactors. There are no Confederate Re-enactors, (of any race), and no references to the Confederate History of Virginia. I have personally checked on this for years. It is like it never happened.) The City of Natchez, Mississippi has a Black Union re-enactor representing the Civil War at their Visitor's Center.

At what point do we draw a line? When do we stand for truth?

Please take the time to investigate for yourself, and write the Governors of the various States that you visit. Bring it to their attention. Let them know what you feel about this kind of censorship. Mention the fact that you are a voter with a big mouth, a large Church, and are active in local politics. They will get your message. If you and your family remain quiet, we will lose this nation. You have to do something. Speak up at Church.

History happened. Studying history does not equate to an acceptance of the behavior or acts of people long-since dead. We did not cause our history to happen, and no one alive today is responsible for anything someone else did 150 to 200 years ago. Do not let anyone convince you that you are liable for the actions of your ancestors. Those who press for apologies from others today are fools, plain and simple. Those politicians who advocate these apologies are arrogant rabble-rousers who have no real answers to real problems. They upset people for votes. They pander for their power. They are not true leaders.

By re-discovering the truth, we all stand to benefit as a people. That discovery is where we must start. Visit museums and battlefields and ask questions. If the answers sound silly, then probe some more. Those Park Service employees are <u>your</u> employees. Demand excellence in their behavior, or seek to cut their funding. When they say "servants", did they mean "slaves"?

Openness is the key:

Years ago, I performed at a large mall in California, and had a conversation with an African-American woman who had a shop there. She began by saying, "God Bless you, Mr. Gipson". She continued by adding that she was nearly 70 years old, and had never heard a White man discuss Black history in public. I was astounded. Was that what I was doing by telling the whole story?

I do not look at this as Black History; I look at this as American History.

At a mall in Jacksonville, North Carolina, an elderly African-American gentleman approached me after a show with tears welling up in his eyes. He wanted to thank me, and this is what he said,

"When I was a young man, my great-grandfather was still alive. He seemed ancient to me, and I loved to listen to his funny stories.

One afternoon, he began to tell us of the time he was in the Confederate Army. We tried to convince him that his memory was gone and that he was in the Union Army. We chided him and joked about his memory. I don't know why I remember this, but I do. Yesterday, I was here in the mall and I heard you talk about the African-Americans who fought with the Confederates. I never heard of this. Mr. Gipson, and I am nearly 71 years old. When I thought about it some more, it made me call my sister and I asked if she had any of his military records. She told me the company he was with, and I looked it up late last night. It was a Confederate Company out of Virginia. I started to cry. All I could think about was how we had made fun of an old man who was trying to tell us the truth. He was in the Confederate Army".

The man shook my hand for nearly a minute. He stared at me again and started to cry. He then turned away and left....shaking his head. I couldn't move...I just felt empty.

It astounds me how Black leaders have taken so much of their own people's history away from them with these cover-ups. I ache for their loss. Omitting history is a covert way of lying. That very mall stopped having our show back because another African-American did not want anything about the Civil War in the mall. Censorship by one hateful individual took away more African-American history to how many more interested Blacks?

I have had the experience of speaking with ignorant and hateful people of all races in the many years on the road as well; I have to add that that wasn't the norm. Usually, the problems came from White males who didn't want to hear any of the flag history, and thought I was just making this up. I was dashing their "fantasy" history, and it hurt. Ignorance recoils at the truth, sometimes.

Most of the audiences I have met and shared stories with are in agreement with my message. I believe that we are still a majority.

We need open conversation; we need to speak with each other. I plan to continue what I am doing for as long as I can. I intend to write more, explore more, and uncover more. I'm having fun.

Remember that a great nation builds itself from within. Legislation, alone, will not succeed; politics only obstruct.

America was a great nation once, and, with the Grace of God, we can grow again. I believe, like others, that we are under assault by people who want our nation to give up its roots and its values. These people have no sense of American Tradition.

God save this Nation. God save the South. I thank all of you for your prayers and thoughts.

"Were it ever to be proposed again to enter into a Union with such a people, I could no more consent to do it than to trust myself in a den of thieves...There is indeed a difference between the two peoples. Let no man hug the delusion that there can be renewed association between them.....

.....Our enemies are...traditionless."
~JEFFERSON DAVIS

FLAGS

ILLUSTRATION I

ILLUSTRATION 2

ILLUSTRATION 3

ILLUSTRATION 4

ILLUSTRATION 5

ILLUSTRATION 6

1: Moultrie Flag

2: 1st Republic of South Carolina

3: 2nd Republic of South Carolina

4: Sovereignty Flag

5: Big Red (CITADEL FLAG)

6: Austrian Flag 1850

ILLUSTRATION 7

ILLUSTRATION 8

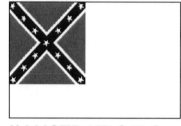

ILLUSTRATION 9

ILLUSTRATION 10

ILLUSTRATION 11 **ILLUSTRATION 12** **ILLUSTRATION 13**

7: Stars and Bars (Ist Issue)   8: Stars and Bars (Last Issue)

9: 2nd National (Stainless Banner)   10: 3rd National Flag

11: Battle Flag (1st Issue)   12: Battle Flag (2nd Issue)

13: Battle Flag (3rd Issue)

ILLUSTRATION 14   **ILLUSTRATION 15**

ILLUSTRATION 16

14: Naval Jack / Army of Tennessee Battle Flag

15: First Confederate Naval Jack

16: Typical Re-Union Color Posting

CHOCTAW NATION

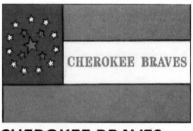

CHEROKEE BRAVES

**SONS OF ERIN, C.S.A.
IRISH**

**EARL VAN DORN TRANS
MISSISSIPPI**

C.S.A. REVENUE SERVICE

HARDEE CORPS

LEE'S HQ. FLAG

S.C. SECESSION FLAG

3RD KENTUCKY MTD.INF.

MAURY'S FLAG

FINALIST FLAG

FINALIST FLAG

There were even more Confederate flags than these; this is the reason why the Army of Tennessee was later ordered to carry the one flag that is so recognizable today, to lessen the confusion.

Over time, we have seen the Confederate Battle Flag displayed over and over again. It is easy to see why we, as Southerners, have lost sight of our past, and all of the other Southern flags.

In today's media, it is always The Confederate Battle Flag that comes up in movies, even though they may not have been used by that army or in that situation. Please… remember…….

HOLLYWOOD MAKES ELEPHANTS FLY!

"It is in their glory that we humble ourselves. What titans they were to sacrifice so much for their beliefs. Lo', that we could ever recapture their strength of character and depth of spirit. We will follow as best we can. Lead on, o' mighty warriors of truth."

Your humble servant, Steve Gipson

ABOUT THE AUTHOR

Steve Gipson has performed nationally since 1975.

He wrote and produced a traveling multi-media show called "America's Fastest Cartoonist" which toured for twenty four years. Combining satire with quick-sketch artistry, he brought humor and political satire together to create a fast-moving, cutting edge comedic act.

He shares his Civil War interest with his wife, Allison, an accomplished artist and actress at their home, Buttonwillow Plantation, in Tennessee. His curiosity and passion for the 19th century manifested itself with a play called "Granddaddy's Watch" which he has produced since 2006.

He continues to research and write about the War Between the States, and will soon author another book on more stories of our American past.

He and Allison appear in person at their theater, The Buttonwillow Civil War Dinner Theater, in Whitwell, Tennessee.

"Yankees," he winked, "are most welcome... but will be closely watched."

"Deo Vindice"